SAFE, SECURE

& FREE

Jeff,
Your beautiful work
is a blessing!
Thank you!
Kelly

KELLY HAWKINS

LifeCare
·Publishing

Copyright © 2019 by Kelly Hawkins

Cover design by Kelly Hawkins.
Cover photo by Jeff Moore.

ISBN- 9781791886356

LifeCare Publishing is a branch of
LifeCare Christian Center
A non-profit faith-based ministry
www.LifeCareChristianCenter.org
info.lifecarecc@gmail.com
Westland, MI USA

Mission Statement

LifeCare Christian Center exists to partner with individuals, churches and the community in promoting spiritual, emotional, physical and relational wholeness by providing quality, affordable care, education and training services from a Christian perspective.

In memory of my brother:

a man who had a tender heart

like Jesus

ACKNOWLEDGMENTS

I am thankful for so many who have impacted my life in beautiful ways as I've worked on this book. There are a few that I would especially like to highlight as they've supported this leg of the journey in some pronounced ways.

Dr. David Atiyeh—my former chiropractor and friend, in certain ways, made this book possible. Sitting at a computer and writing for hundreds of hours is not SAFE—it takes a toll on the body. He put me back together routinely while pouring out love, support and encouragement in authentic friendship. I miss you much, Dr. A!

Lillian—thank you for so many life-lessons as you've walked with me to understand this topic. Thank you for sharing beautiful friendship with me and for giving me a living example of what it is to live safe, secure & free in relationship and in life. And the fact that you're one of my biggest cheerleaders warms my heart beyond words!

Tiffanie—your gentle, persistent, loving inquiries about when this book would be finished motivated me to keep working. Thanks for loving my writing!

Jeff Moore—you are an amazing photographer! Thank you for your generosity with your beautiful work.

Robbie and Kristi—thank you for your stories that gave substance to some of my topics. And thank you for always making me feel safe, secure and free in your presence.

Maureen—thank you for your careful and caring approach to proofing these pages... quickly! I so appreciate you!

My husband and kids—I'm grateful for your patience, understanding and support as you've rolled with late dinners and late nights because I was on a roll. And thanks for giving me breaks to laugh and play. Allison—thank you for desiring to use your amazing editing skills on this book. It delights me that you delight in my work.

I'm thankful for all those (and there are so many of you) who have cheered me on and longed to read this book (friends, family, fellow authors, ministry leaders)—you have strengthened me more than I can express!

I am so thankful to God for giving me a voice through writing, topics that He's put in my heart and life to talk about, amazing life-lessons that have transformed me, and the skills needed for writing, publishing and everything in between. It delights me that He's equipped me and given me immense freedom to live out my calling.

CONTENTS

FOREWORD

I WOULD LIKE TO ENCOURAGE YOU before you read the following pages to enter into a mindset and heart position that is prayed up and open to receive a strong touch of conviction as well as a beautiful tender touch from God through Kelly's words. You may be challenged with a new perspective on what it means to be safe, secure and free, and if so, I ask you to consider all that you have read and allow the truth to penetrate your own soul just as hers has been touched and changed.

SAFE, SECURE & FREE is not a book to rush through. Each chapter has words to savor and meditate on. Take your time, enjoy the journey, and more importantly, use Kelly's experiences with God to draw you closer to His heart where you experience what it means to be delighted in, deeply loved and accepted. This is a book you will want to share with others and re-visit as you grow in your relationship with Christ.

–Lillian Easterly-Smith
Founder & Director, LifeCare Christian Center

AN ANCHOR

"We have this hope as an anchor for our
lives, safe and secure."
–Hebrews 6.19, HCSB

I had the opportunity to go to Chicago in January for a week of solitude and writing. My preference would have been someplace warm, but I had been hoping to get away to work on this book, so I jumped at the opportunity since the accommodations were free, the travel expenses were minimal and it fit with my schedule. I left on a Wednesday and returned home the following Wednesday. I knew the presidential inauguration would be two days after I arrived, but I didn't anticipate anything about it that would impact my time there, and that was accurate.

My best work is accomplished late at night, resulting in me sleeping late into the morning (roughly 2 or 3am–10 or 11am), but Saturday morning, my third morning there, many street noises nudged my awareness—noises out of the ordinary. After a couple hours of being determined to not allow the noises of whistles, sirens and helicopters to disrupt my rest, curiosity drew me to my cell phone to explore possible events in the area.

What I found was that the entire country (actually the entire world—how I was out of the loop on that one, I'm not sure) was gathering in various locations (predominantly Washington D.C., with more than 600 sister marches across the country and throughout the world drawing millions) to rally and march for women's rights. To some extent, there were those who also came to protest the incoming president. The march in Chicago was initially expected to draw roughly 22,000 people, but officials canceled the march and restricted it to just a rally when more than 250,000 people showed up in downtown Chicago to gather in Grant Park (three blocks from my hotel).

The entire day (and weekend), the news and social media were saturated with the event and people's strong opinions regarding women's rights, rallying, protesting, etc. I found myself unsettled. So, I did what I do when I'm unsettled—I asked God about it. What I began to understand was that so many people in this country are reacting, maybe not so much because they simply feel strongly about something, but because they don't feel safe in living out the lives they hope to live; they don't feel secure in their environment; and they don't feel free to be who they believe they are.

When someone doesn't feel safe, they may act out. The acting out may look more like aggression, demandingness, disrespect and control, but it's hard to see beneath the surface when actions are so explicit. But there is a deeper need—sometimes physical, oftentimes emotional—and an understanding person is often able to reach those deeper places with compassion, sensitivity and care that paves a path toward safety, security and freedom—a path we need to both provide for others and receive ourselves.

I thought it was quite fitting that I was writing *Safe, Secure & Free* in the midst of this Chicago event. My longing in writing and compiling these pages is to give all people (regardless of political affiliation, gender, race or identity) hope that experiencing safety, security and freedom is possible.

IT REALLY IS POSSIBLE

When I first read John Eldredge's first book, *Sacred Romance*, my view of God being safe for me became disrupted. About the same time, a quote by C. S. Lewis in *The Lion, the Witch and the Wardrobe*, also troubled me:

"…he isn't safe. But he's good."

I needed Aslan, a representation of God, to be good AND safe.

A mentor prayed for me that God would show me what I needed to know about Him being safe. Fifteen years later I began writing this book because I had grown to understand and experience God's safety, which is so much more astonishing than our general comprehension of it.

A FIRM FOUNDATION

Why is it even important to be safe and secure—to have the *experience* of being safe and secure? And why do I need to be free?

The ultimate goal, and our biblical calling, should always be to pursue what leads to loving God and loving others. Safety and security give us a firm foundation so that we can be grounded, and then we are more equipped and empowered to freely love God and love others.

When I first got married, within six weeks of our wedding, my husband hit a busy season with work which required him to work around 70 hours a week for three or four months (and this happened annually). We were also very involved in ministry. I found myself feeling very insecure with my husband. When he would come home from work, and we had an event to go to, I found myself clinging to him rather than freely reaching out to love others, not knowing when I would be able to have time with him again. Recognizing what was happening, we decided to commit to a date night every week. That way I confidently knew that I would always have at least one evening each week to spend with him. The result was that it freed me up when we were with other people to be able to love on them, knowing that I would have time with my husband at some given point.

Safety and security became "an anchor for my life" and gave me freedom to embrace God's calling on my life, to be who He created me to be, to love others and to fulfill my purpose in this life.

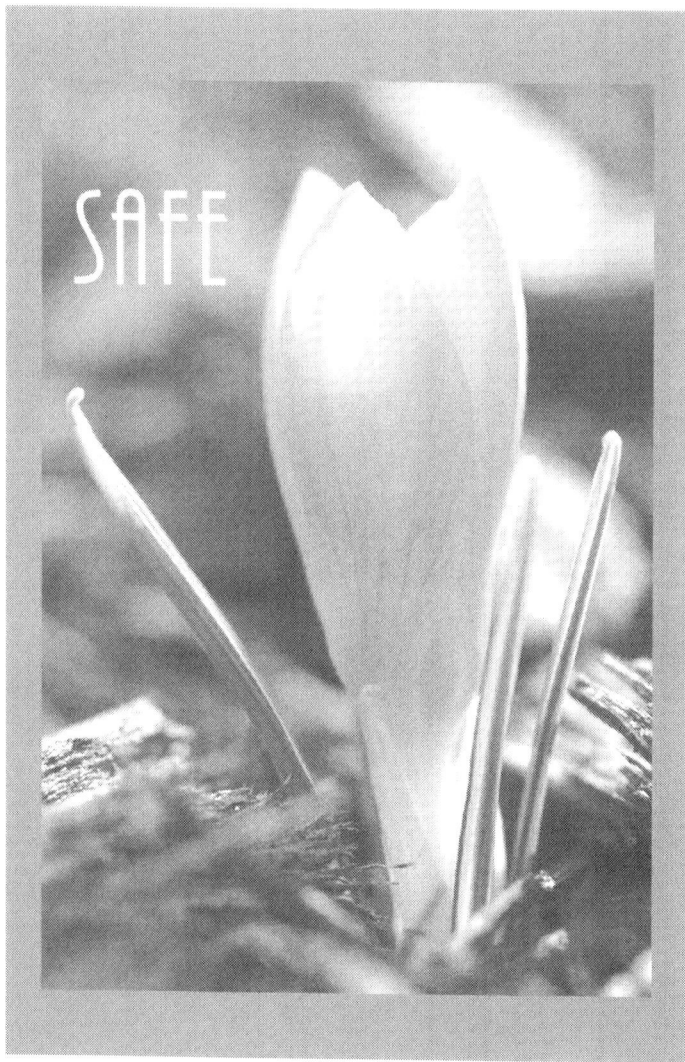

SAFE

safe
[sāf]

ADJECTIVE
1.   protected from or not exposed to danger or risk; not likely to be harmed or lost.

...

6.b.   trustworthy, reliable

Also:

Safety is having an environment of understanding and support, free from physical or emotional attack. Sometimes with challenge of character or actions, but always with an attitude of love.

1

I'M A RUNNER

"Run in such a way as to get the prize."
–1 Corinthians 9.24b

*N*ow granted, I have put on running shoes and actually run a mile or two at times—once I even ran a 10K that about killed me, but I'm not *really* a runner in the sense of exercise. I would say I'm definitely a runner in the sense of escape—either running to something or away from something. Sometimes I run TO something because I enjoy it and/or I'm called to it; other times I run TO something in order to run AWAY from something else.

Life can be hard and feel unsafe. Sometimes I look for relief because I don't know how to deal with something I'm facing—or maybe "should be" facing.

My marriage was struggling. I knew I had a part in the struggle, but it was overwhelming, and I had no idea where to start or how to approach it. I know I have a tendency toward avoidance when I feel like that, but we always run to something when we run away. Sometimes it's sleep, because I do feel extra tired when I'm running. Sometimes it's work. Sometimes it's both, where I work half of the night and sleep half of the day. Maybe it's running to a friend excessively. Maybe it's running to another relationship for intimacy—or possibly running to another relationship just in my thoughts. Sometimes it's food or any sort of activity—even good things.

But the important question is "Am I running away from something?" When any part of life doesn't feel safe, I have an exceptional ability to run in the opposite direction of the thing that doesn't feel safe; often, that thing has something to do with other people. I don't like that about myself—that I have anxiety and fear that can drive me to my "running shoes." Because of that tendency, I'm continually working toward building greater strength and courage where there are battles to be fought, and pursuing truth, healing and trust in God in the areas where my thoughts and feelings deceive me or overwhelm me.

My desire is for God to take my ability to run and channel it into a race to run for His glory—to run toward the plan that He has laid out for my life—with all the obstacles, inclement weather and even people who try to trip me up at times. And in that race, I want to run in such a way that I would be the winner. I want the prize at the end, and the confidence of knowing that the way I ran gave God the most glory that He could possibly get from my life.

FULLY INVESTED

I look at how Jesus ran. He ran toward people; He used all the energy He had to align Himself with His Father's desire: He loved His Father and He loved the people His Father created. God's desire is for intimate connection with each one of us, and despite many obstacles and "impossibilities", Jesus paved the way for God's love to run to us.

"And we know that in all things God works for the good of those who love him, who have been called according to his purpose." (Romans 8.28)

I guess I've believed that the above verse meant that God's hands surrounded my childhood and my entire life. I still do believe that; however, I believe that it's more than that. Where I once only saw God's hands surrounding my life like this:

I now see that He ran right into my life—His hands were open, fingers outstretched with His hands and fingers interwoven throughout my childhood and my life, working it all for good.

It makes a difference. He's not just in control and sovereign over my life; He's FULLY INVESTED IN IT. When we have confidence in His sovereignty, good interconnection and intervention in our lives, it creates an environment where we can be still—where we can rest (even as we work).

Words in the song, "Still", by Hillsong say:

Hide me now under Your wings...
When the oceans rise and thunders roar
I will soar with you above the storm
Father, You are King over the flood
I will be still and know You are God.

We are in an unsafe world. Because of that, as we live fully in the world, we need God's protection. We have purpose within the dangers of the world—not to be taken out of the danger or threat of harm, but to be protected within it, as we display His attributes: His strength, power, and love. We must have peace and be able to be still to truly manifest His love IN the danger.

2

THE CARNIVAL

"'In this world you will have trouble. But
take heart! I have overcome the world.'"
–John 16.33b

O n the back of this section's title page, I have
the definition of "Safe". It's something I
wrestled with for years until I finally began to
understand it from God's perspective.

Even in the Bible, we clearly see that this world is not
safe. Jesus Himself said, "'I have told you these things, so
that in me you may have peace. In this world you will
have trouble. But take heart! I have overcome the
world.'" (John 16.33) It seems that people are attacking
each other in various ways every day. Tragedy is
rampant. If we go a day without hearing of a tragedy, it
almost seems like we've missed something.

Even Jesus wasn't exempt from the tragedy of this
world, but He never considered this His Home. Take a
look at His perspective here as He was aware that it

wouldn't be long before He would be returning to His true Home:

> The Lord Jesus, on the night he was betrayed, took bread, and when he had given thanks, he broke it and said, "This is my body, which is for you; do this in remembrance of me." (I Corinthians 11.23b-24)

Notice that it says, "on the night he was '**betrayed**'". It doesn't say on the night he was arrested or accused or even handed over (all of which are true). Instead, it says betrayed. That doesn't sound safe to me. Yet, He was still able to give of Himself for the benefit of the others—and not just ANY others—it specifically included the one who betrayed Him. He poured out His life for each of His disciples, for each of us, for everyone He created, including Judas—one that He invited in and welcomed into His inner circle—one that He taught and fed and discipled—one whose feet He washed.

I was reading in the book of Luke not long ago. Jesus was there and...

> ...when a crowd of many thousands had gathered, so that they were trampling on one another, Jesus began to speak first to his disciples, saying:
> "Be on your guard against the yeast of the Pharisees, which is hypocrisy. ...I tell you, my

friends, do not be afraid of those who kill the body and after that can do no more. But I will show you whom you should fear: Fear him who, after your body has been killed, has authority to throw you into hell. Yes, I tell you, fear him. Are not five sparrows sold for two pennies? Yet not one of them is forgotten by God. Indeed, the very hairs of your head are all numbered. Don't be afraid; you are worth more than many sparrows." (Luke 12.1, 4-7)

Wait! Did He really say, "Do not be afraid of those who kill the body and after that can do no more"???

GOD KNOWS SOMETHING THAT WE DON'T

We value this life, don't we? I believe God values it; yet, we value it as if there's nothing else. I guess since it's all we've ever known, it kind of makes sense; but God knows something that we don't. He has the entire overview; He sees the big picture; He's on top of the mountain and has perfect perspective.

"Do not be afraid of those who kill the body...." Those who kill the body? Well, unfortunately these days, that sounds like some of our inner-city streets, some of our neighborhoods, some of our schools, and even terrorists, but it also sounds like cancer and many other diseases that threaten to kill the body. Many of us—I'd even venture to say most of us—value this body—this life—as if there's nothing else. Don't get me wrong, we should value this body and care for it well—it is the temple of the Holy Spirit for those who've received Jesus. And I certainly strive to make my temple a delightful dwelling place for the Holy Spirit.

So what did Jesus mean by not being afraid of those who kill the body?

I picture a huge carnival—a party thrown by God just for you. You are there celebrating with pony rides, hot air balloon rides, bungee jumping, all kinds of carnival rides, carnival games, festive music (even your favorite band playing in your honor), balloons all over the place, cotton candy and elephant ears (kinds that taste amazing but aren't bad for you, of course), and party favors—all to celebrate and honor you!

> THE ONLY THING HE HAS THE POWER TO DO IS TO POP ONE BALLOON

And then Satan, our enemy, comes along to crash the party, but the only thing he has power to do is to pop one balloon. That one balloon represents this body in this life. But the carnival continues. God wants us to understand that we are His creation of body, soul and spirit, and that there's so much more beyond this body in this life.

So how do we respond?

"Do not be afraid of those who kill the body and after that can do no more." When our lives are hidden in

Christ, the body is the only thing the enemy has access to. Certainly, every loss is sad, but the point is to not let it steal the joy of the entire carnival. And certainly, don't let the anticipation of loss steal your joy. Your safety is in the hands of the One who holds all the rest of the carnival. There's something so much bigger and better and more extravagant than what we can see right now!

HIS WINGS

We can understand that there's an amazing carnival of our existence that God intends to bring to fruition. And we can know that His

THE DARKER OUR SURROUNDINGS SEEM, THE MORE TIGHTLY GOD'S WINGS ARE PRESSING INTO US AND COVERING US TO

plans for us are for good, with His plans interwoven through our entire lives. Still, the dark places can feel intimidating. In those times, we can take comfort knowing that He hides us in the shadow of His wings, just like a mother bird protecting her young. We can also know that the darker our surroundings seem, the more tightly God's wings are pressing into us and covering us to protect us.

I was reading Psalm 91 this morning. Powerful. If you want stability and security in your life, you have to get into God's Word.

"Those who live in the shelter of the Most High will find rest in the shadow of the Almighty." (Psalm 91.1, NLT)

In this life, there are difficulties that we need shelter from. There is chaos and work and turmoil and things that constantly wear on us so that we need rest. If we live in Him, He will be our protector; we will be sheltered and able to rest in His shadow. But there can be no shadow without light. Know that even when darkness surrounds us, there is light in His presence.

THE TENDER HEART OF GOD

> "He tends his flock like a shepherd: He
> gathers the lambs in his arms and carries
> them close to his heart; he gently leads
> those that have young."
> –Isaiah 40.11

As a parent, I've always wanted to keep my kids safe. But the burden of that responsibility can feel overwhelming at times. As I read this verse, I sense a strong, sovereign companion assuming ultimate responsibility. It feels freeing. The ultimate burden is lifted from my shoulders and my husband's shoulders and placed on God's.

When it says, "He gently leads those that have young", I can have confidence that He's gently leading me as well as my husband. And when it says, "He gathers the lambs in his arms and carries them close to his heart", I can have confidence that He has our kids in His own hands and carries them close to His heart. He has a tender heart for my kids and is constantly drawing them to Himself.

That reassurance is so comforting and helps me feel safe and secure in His care.

3

HOW TO BE A CHILD

"Jesus called a little one to his side and
said to [the disciples], 'Learn this well:
Unless you dramatically change your way
of thinking and become teachable, and
learn about heaven's kingdom realm with
the wide-eyed wonder of a child, you will
never be able to enter in. Whoever
continually humbles himself to become
like this gentle child is the greatest one in
heaven's kingdom realm.'"
–Matthew 18.2-4, TPT

God: *"You've been learning to be a grown-up
for 40 years; now I want to teach you to be a
child."*

Yesterday that sounded refreshing. But today, I
realized… a child is dependent!

Me: "God, Your Word talks about You being a Father, but right now I need You to be a mother to me."

God: *"I can do that, but you need to know how to be a child."*

Me: "What is a child?"

God: *"A child is...*
- *dependent on her caregivers for food, loving discipline, to clean her up, etc.*
- *to follow the guidance of her caregivers.*
- *to be meek (fire, beauty and passion submitted to Christ).*
- *able to enjoy the moment and not worry about the future.*
- *always looking for what's good in whatever circumstances she's in—to find and enjoy the land flowing with milk and honey."*

THE MOTHER BIRD

I feel ambivalent about the image of the mother bird (image in previous chapter) with the two little ones under her wings. In one sense, I love it, but I also wrestle with it. I want to trust that God is that kind of nurturer and protector for me, and I also desire that and want to trust it in human interaction, but that kind of trust can be scary.

Most of us have been betrayed at some point where we should have received care and/or protection—whether by a parent, a teacher, a coach, a pastor, or some other care-provider or authority figure. It feels vulnerable to be in that "receiving" position though—protected in one sense, yet dependent on "the mother bird" and vulnerable to her to protect us and care for us well.

If I'm under someone else's care and protection, I depend on that person. When trust has previously been betrayed, that kind of dependence can be scary. If I'm fearful, I'm not able to rest in the protection and care; I'll be aware and vigilant about it—watching for cues regarding whether or not that "mother bird" will protect me and care for me at any given time or in any given situation.

The fear may be that she'll forget to care for me, especially when she gets busy with work, ministry, other people—life. I may fear that she'll forget about caring for my needs, or worse yet, that she won't care about my needs. Or that she'll put someone in my place under her wing and neglect me—maybe someone she thinks needs her more—or someone new and more interesting or exciting. Maybe she'll even consider my needs too difficult to deal with and choose to distance herself from them. Those have been some of my beliefs, but God spoke to me about them.

God: "I chose those who care for you and who have cared for you. They blow it and do fall short at times, but I always fill in the gaps that need to be filled.

"Their shortcomings are not my intention, but I will use them for good in your life—to do amazing things beyond your comprehension. Look what I did in Joseph's life. His father coddled him and didn't require him to work to be a strong man—so physically and emotionally he was weak. Even spiritually he hadn't learned how to depend on Me. He had a spiritual foundation, but it was weak. I built his strength: spiritually as he learned to turn to Me in his desperate circumstances, physically as he had to endure a slave's treatment, and emotionally as he faced a hard world that didn't protect him, yet he knew I would."

Me: "That's where I get hung up. It doesn't look to me like You protected him."

God: "I allowed him to reap the consequences of pride so he would learn how to choose to be humble. I allowed him to reap the consequences of someone else's poor choices so he would know compassion, kindness, patience—the fruit of the spirit—and My sovereignty. He grew strong emotionally."

Me: "So what do You want to do with me?"

God: *"I want you to trust Me with the imperfect people I have in your life. Others don't always know your needs, but I always know your needs and I've always got your back. When you're desperate for Me, I'm always enough. You tend to get desperate for someone or something else though."*

Me: "I get desperate for someone or something else because I feel empty and hungry—and there are others who give me a taste of what I hunger for—a nurturer who understands me and will delight in me and love me well according to my love languages."

God: *"You get desperate when you don't trust these things you know about Me. Your trust is growing though. Keep leaning into Me, and I will keep showing you my heart."*

4

WATERS OF LIFE

"'Peace! Be still!' And the wind ceased,
and there was a great calm."
–Mark 4.39b, ESV

"'*P*eace! Be still!'" He commanded with clear resolve. And then there was stillness.

I spent many summer days of my childhood with my grandparents at their lake property where they stayed in a small travel trailer, and I slept in my tent when I visited. It was a pretty rustic setting with a hand-pump well for drinking water, and an outhouse at the top of the hill. It was unusual, but I think that made that time in my life even more special.

I would wake up early, before the sun burned the morning mist off the lake. I would climb into the little rowboat with my grandpa, and we would row out onto the lake in an attempt to catch some fish. Of all the times we went out like this, I really can't remember if we caught anything. What stands out in my memory is the stillness of the water in that peaceful time—just my grandpa and me. He was a tall man, strong and sturdy. He protected me and gave me many opportunities to experience the fullness of life. And in that fullness, all the waters of life were stilled when I was with him.

TURBULENCE

John 6:16-21, NLT says,

> That evening Jesus' disciples went down to the shore to wait for him. But as darkness fell and Jesus still hadn't come back, they got into the boat and headed out across the lake toward Capernaum. Soon a gale swept down upon them, and the sea grew very rough. They had rowed three or four miles when suddenly they saw Jesus walking on the water toward the boat. They were terrified, but he called out to them, "Don't be afraid. I am here!" Then they were eager to let him in the boat, and immediately they arrived at their destination!

What I noticed is that their circumstances got rough. Then Jesus showed up. They were three or four miles out from where they had been as well as three or four miles from Capernaum—their destination, and seeing a figure on the water scared them until they realized it was Jesus. They let him in the boat and then they were immediately on shore.

As I read this, it's mind-boggling. It's impossible. But I wonder if God reached down under the water, using the turbulence He had just stilled, and had swept His hand under the boat creating a huge wave that set them on the shore immediately.

As I consider this for my own life, just yesterday I looked at a situation in my life and told my husband that it just flat out is not going to change. I had no hope

I HAD NO HOPE FOR CHANGE

for change in the situation that looked completely impossible—just like it is impossible for people to arrive at a destination three or four miles away in about two seconds.

Maybe, then, it could be the turbulence in my life that is actually His hand moving under my life stirring things up so that He can do an impossible thing.

DELIGHTED

My grandpa loved the water, and he loved to give me the experience of being out on the water. I don't think it mattered whether or not we caught fish; I think he just delighted in being with his granddaughter.

I think God is the same way. Whether He is sitting with us in a peaceful time or showing up in the midst of turmoil—whatever the situation, He delights in us wherever we are. I love this excerpt from the book, *Tattoos on the Heart:*

> Where we stand, in all our mistakes and imperfection, is holy ground. It is where God has chosen to be intimate with us and not in any way but this. Scrappy's moment of truth was not in recognizing what a disappointment he's been all these years. It came in realizing that God had been beholding him and smiling for all this time, unable to look anywhere else.

I think that's what God's love is like—love that makes you forget that you're flawed.

5

THE MOUNTAIN TOP

"He lifted me out of the slimy pit, out of
the mud and mire; he set my feet on a rock
and gave me a firm place to stand."
–Psalm 40.2

I am staying in a chalet at a ski resort on a mountain. Sounds dreamy, doesn't it? I don't ski and didn't intend to be outside much; I came to write. Knowing what my plan was for writing, I also had in mind what kind of environment I desired. But knowing that God knows better than I do about what I need, I asked Him to provide His best choice for me.

Well, knowing the kind of wise, loving provider that He is, I should have known better than to anticipate luxury and perfection. I've learned over and over that just because I get what I want doesn't mean I'll be satisfied. I confess, I kind of anticipated that He would give me large, second-floor, beautiful accommodations, maybe with a hot tub, a view of majestic mountains where I could watch skiers riding the lift up the mountain and then swooshing all the way down the mountain as I sat in warm luxury, alternating my gaze between my computer screen, the constant glow of the fireplace and the picturesque view. Ahhh...

I checked in yesterday and was told that my unit would be on the first floor. Hmm... slightly disappointed, but still anticipating the many blessings to come, I made my way to God's best choice for me. I swiped my key card in the outside door which opened to A and B doors. B was mine, so I swiped my card again, and pushed the door open with excitement, and was overcome with a weight that pulled my bags to the floor and drew tears from my eyes. There had to be a mistake! I hate cupboards that are painted blue, but this is what I would have for the next three days. It felt small, no hot tub, décor that resembled the 60's, a view of the parking lot, and... a fireplace that could only be on for 30 minutes at a time until it cooled down to be manually turned on again.

Why wouldn't God come through for me? He came through for me last week when He gave me the words I needed for a difficult conversation. So why not this time?

After wallowing in self-pity for about 60 seconds (okay, well, maybe 120), it hit me that THIS WAS God's best for me. In His wisdom, He knew what I needed to hear from Him regarding this book (and my life). I knew that He had something special for me in these exact circumstances, in this exact place. So I chose to be attentive to His voice and watch for whatever way He wanted to speak to me.

This afternoon I went out for a walk. It was a brisk 34 degrees, but sunny with a beautiful blue sky. I turned on my walking app on my phone and began walking down the sidewalk in front of the other units. I got a quick glimpse of the ski slope around the corner of my building (and a glimpse of attitude in my heart) but kept walking "down" the sidewalk. I noticed that it was going down in elevation. As I kept walking toward the next set of units, I noticed I was whispering to myself things like, "Oh, I'm glad they didn't give me one of those units; they have no view at all." "I'm glad I'm not there; they're literally looking into their neighbor's building." "I'm glad I'm not there; they only have tall weeds to look at, but I suppose if I were, I could hear from God through that." Hmm. I kept walking and noticed a small stream that came up to the side of the road and circled back and out of sight. It was beautiful with the clean, white, melting snow gently reaching over the bank with the bright, blue sky as the backdrop that hugged the young trees that swayed in the gentle breeze. I stopped to take a picture and breathe in the refreshment.

I turned to walk back toward my chalet, and noticed the elevation from which I'd come. I could see my home-away-from-home high up—actually the highest of all the units in the area. It looked almost majestic. I realized that, from my unit and elevation, I could look out across my parking lot and see for miles—I had just been distracted by the parking lot and hadn't noticed.

I recognized that sometimes in life we are in a valley, and we look up and see so much that's beautiful and wish we were there. In that valley, we can lose sight of the amazing provision God has for us in that place as we long for more beauty. The longing is from God as He created us for Eden and the eternal future He intends for us. But sometimes the longing is for luxury now, or in my case this week, to live in luxury AND look up at God's beauty. I had wanted to look up at the mountain, but God chose to put me up ON the mountain to look out over His creation. The view is different.

WHAT LOOKS ORDINARY FROM ABOVE LOOKS MAJESTIC FROM BELOW

Sometimes I do a little bit of very amateur photography. If you've ever been with me when I'm taking pictures, you know that I often stoop down low to get under an image. Look at a flower from that perspective. What looks ordinary from above looks majestic from below. Imagine being small enough to be ON the flower and look out across the landscape—different perspective.

So God has placed me, for these few days, on His mountain of privilege to gain more of His perspective. Where I was disappointed yesterday, today I'm honored. It's a visual reminder of the privilege I have in His presence every day because He is holding me up, securely in His hand.

The verse at the beginning of this chapter says the following in another translation:

"He pulled me out of a dangerous pit, out of the deadly quicksand. He set me safely on a rock and made me secure." –Psalm 40.2 (GNT)

One other thing that stood out to me in this scenario was recognizing how God empowers us with strength and influence in our world. We can choose to lift ourselves up, but if I elevate myself and look down on others, I'll only see darkness and dreariness. But if I stoop down and elevate others, I capture a more stunning glimpse of their beauty.

In order to stoop down and elevate them, I may ask myself:

- What can I do and say to speak and breathe life into others?
- What do they need from me?
- How can I build them up?

...not focusing on my own weaknesses, inhibitions, insecurities, but rather on how I can benefit them.

6

UNIDENTIFIED BAGGAGE

"'They have eyes to see but do not see
and ears to hear but do not hear....'"
–Ezekiel 12.2b

She was well-dressed and well-groomed, although I probably wouldn't have noticed. She walked with a notable confidence, not entirely common of women exiting a waiting room bathroom.

I was engrossed in a book, my head lowered toward the pages, when my eyes glimpsed the bright white train flowing so freely from her heel as she passed in front of me. Maybe it wouldn't have been so noticeable had it not been for the rather dark colored décor and adequate lighting of the orthodontist's office.

Only one other person was in the room—a man obviously aware of the sight. I could tell he was aware because of his sudden stillness. He sat uncomfortably motionless as only his eyes inconspicuously followed the

THE WOMAN DISAPPEARED AND WILL LIKELY NEVER KNOW HER IMPACT ON HER WORLD

train. Then it happened. The train broke loose and sat in a bundle directly in front of him.

The woman disappeared and will likely never know her impact on her world, nor will she ever recognize the baggage she once dragged behind. But we'll get to that thought in a bit.

The man in the room continued to sit quite uncomfortably. I was uncomfortable. There was tension in the room, but neither of us was willing to acknowledge the toilet paper...or each other for that matter. It was a bit more comfortable to pretend we knew nothing about the toilet paper.

Several people walked through the room, stepping around or over it. Eventually, a woman gracefully passed by, picked it up and threw it away. Amazingly, all the tension immediately left the room.

There are times when someone crosses our path with baggage so blatant that it makes everyone uncomfortable, except the person himself who is oblivious to it, but reacts to everyone with his, "What's wrong with you?" attitude. I'm thinking of a man I knew who had serious anger issues. He would behave with rude impatience with nearly every interaction and then respond to the stares around him with, "What's your problem!?" He was blind and clueless with no hope for change until he could see his own toilet paper train.

Some toilet paper trains get left in the room leaving its witnesses uncomfortable... and sometimes wounded. People can leave a profound impact and never even realize the train they dragged behind.

As I continued to sit in the waiting room, writing these notes, a mom came in with her daughter. They sat down, but within a couple minutes, the daughter got up to get a magazine. Immediately, the mom said to her daughter, "Come here! You have a Band-Aid stuck on you." The daughter, looking horrified, squealed, "Ew!!" and quickly pealed it off the leg of her pants.

When we're able to see our baggage—our own toilet paper trains dragging behind us or Band-Aids stuck to us, or at least the impact our baggage has, then we're finally able to address it and let God remove it from us. Sometimes we need the insight of others in letting us know when they see some excess baggage stuck on us.

BLIND "UNTIL" I SEE

I've been blind at times, and I'm sure my blindness has inadvertently hurt others. Sometimes people can be blind to some of their shortcomings and as a result they can hurt others.

When I'm the one that is hurt by others' shortcomings that they're not able to see, a part of me desperately wants to get them to see it—for their own sake, for the sake of others, and for my own sake. My attempts at getting them to see something like this often tend to result in frustration on both parts.

In Isaiah 42.16, God says,

I will lead the blind by ways they have not known, along unfamiliar paths I will guide them; I will turn the darkness into light before them and make the rough places smooth. These are the things I will do; I will not forsake them.

The wording in this verse intrigues me. God "will lead the blind" and "guide them" on "unfamiliar paths". This sounds very gentle and patient. He sheds light while making "rough places smooth." I hear a lot of grace in this.

I'm grateful for His patient and gentle guidance as He leads me through my blindness back into light.

7

"I DON'T WANT FUNCTIONAL;
I WANT BEAUTIFUL"

"'Didn't I tell you that you would see God's
glory if you believe?'"
–John 11.40b, NLT

reat Are You, Lord" was on the radio when I
pulled into my driveway.

I like the song musically, and yet some of
the words this particular day were irritating to me—like,
"Great are You, Lord."

I pulled into my garage and started journaling...

My heart is broken... You've left me in
darkness. The song says, "You bring light to the
darkness. You give hope. You restore every heart
that is broken." That makes me angry. I feel
mocked! You're crushing me!

"Our hearts will cry, these bones will sing,
'Great are You, Lord!'"

...WHY?!?!?! "Bones" represent loss of life, DEATH, lack of breath in our lungs.

"It's Your breath in our lungs, so we pour out our praise...."

You're mocking me! I'm angry with You for the suffering I feel that appears to be causing a sort of death in what was functional in my life.

Then I heard God's reply:

"I don't want functional; I want beautiful. I don't want you to just get by; I want you to thrive.

"Where there is death of the old, there can be resurrection of the new. Where I bring resurrection to new life, that new life is something different—it contains something better, more beautiful, more powerful, healed, redeemed, free."

Joseph suffered in prison but was faithful in the darkness while God put the functional to death and brought strength, power and redemption to life.

Trusting God with death brings redemption and freedom. Hebrews 9.15b (NLT) says, "Christ died to set them free...."

In John 11.40b (NLT), Jesus says to Martha regarding the death of Lazarus: "'Didn't I tell you that you would see God's glory if you believe?'"

Lazarus had previously been sick (bondage), but Jesus called him to resurrected life and told the others, "'Unwrap him and let him go!'" (John 11.44b,

NLT)... releasing him not only from his grave clothes, but also from the sickness and bondage he had previously lived with. When Jesus raised Lazarus, He set him free from what caused his death.

Philippians 3:10-11, CEB

"The righteousness that I have comes from knowing Christ, the power of his resurrection, and the participation in his sufferings. It includes being conformed to his death so that I may perhaps reach the goal of the resurrection of the dead."

Philippians 3:10-11, MSG

"I gave up all that inferior stuff so I could know Christ personally, experience his resurrection power, be a partner in his suffering, and go all the way with him to death itself. If there was any way to get in on the resurrection from the dead, I wanted to do it."

I think He's trying to show me that He really is FOR ME. He's building my trust again so we can tackle the bondage, and so He can bring light to the darkness.

I finished writing in my journal that night:

Like Lazarus, maybe I was "sick" for some time and then in the grave for the four days leading up to last night. It sure felt like it inside.

Once again I can sing, "Great are You Lord."

"The resurrected King is resurrecting me!"

PAINFUL WOUNDS

The other day I was introduced to someone, and it was appropriate to reach out and shake the person's hand. I happened to have hurt my right hand the day before and it was very sensitive. As I reached out to shake this person's hand, I was tentative—fearful of my wounded hand being touched or squeezed too tightly and it made me reluctant to freely embrace the other person's hand.

I realized that when I've been emotionally wounded, I become cautious about someone touching my wound or even getting close to it, and I behave differently than when I'm healed. I was able to be functional in my actions, but not beautiful. As I let God heal those wounded places, I'm then able to reach out confidently, focused on the other person rather than my own pain—and respond with beauty.

8

DOLPHINS

"You will keep in perfect peace those
whose minds are steadfast, because they
trust in you." –Isaiah 26:3

*I*f you can just keep your head above the
surface, even intermittently, you feel a tiny bit
of hope for security.

I learned that dolphins, being mammals living in the
water, have to breathe every 6-7 minutes. But they also
require sleep. God, in His magnificent design, created the
dolphin in such a way that it could sleep by shutting
down half of its brain but also continue to come to the
surface for air every 6 to 7 minutes by using the awake
half of the brain for cognizance of this need.

God knew the dilemma that the dolphin would face
while having both the need to sleep and the need to
breathe while living underwater.

I remember a time when, by letting go of my
emotional security blankets, I felt like I wouldn't be able

to breathe and I would literally die. I remember the desperation for God to provide every breath I breathed, and that if He didn't come through for me, I wouldn't survive—I couldn't survive. Day after day for a long season, I would collapse on my bedroom floor, determined to not return to my security blanket but also determined to hold tightly to Jesus—confident that He was my source of hope.

And He was! He was actually holding tightly to me. He brought me through that long season—a season of desperation—a season where I learned that there is a beautiful gift in desperation for God. Not something to be ashamed of, but rather something that gives safety, security and freedom. The dolphin is dependent on God for every breath in order to sleep, and in that dependence, the dolphin has peace. In the same way, we can also live in hope of peace as we remain desperate for and dependent on our God who designed us perfectly and cares for us perfectly.

Matthew 6:26 says:

Look at the birds of the air; they do not sow or reap or store away in barns, and yet your heavenly Father feeds them. Are you not much more valuable than they?

And Psalm 104:25, 27-28:

There is the sea, vast and spacious, teeming with creatures beyond number—living things both large and small. All creatures look to you to give them their food at the proper time. When you give it to them, they gather it up; when you open your hand, they are satisfied with good things.

YOUR EAR ON GOD'S HEART

Do you feel desperate? Desperation can take you to the heart of God. Have you ever used a stethoscope to hear someone's heart? Or put your ear on someone's chest to hear their heartbeat? Then when they speak, it about blows your eardrum because you can hear them so well in that position. Do you want to hear God? Don't hate the desperation, but view it as a gift that can usher you to the heart of God—with your ear on His heart.

THE SWING

LifeCare does healing weekends several times each year. On one of our weekends, during our break, I went for a walk down toward the lake. As I looked for a place to sit, I saw a swing hanging from a branch in a large tree. It looked very inviting and had a wonderful view of the lake, but as I walked closer, I wasn't convinced it would actually be safe to sit on. The wood was weathered and the chains holding it up were small. Both issues aroused a question in my mind as to its ability to hold me. I also questioned whether or not the branch was strong enough to hold me.

Under the swing was packed-down dirt that gave me some confidence that people had actually used the swing fairly often. So I decided to take the risk.

Do you think I jumped right on, threw myself back and tried to swing as high as I possibly could, like a second grader getting underdogs on a playground?

No way. I thought it was possible that it was safe, but I was going to test it cautiously first. I walked up to it, touched the wood to make sure it didn't fall apart, and then very gently and slowly sat down on the edge. It held me. Very gradually, as it demonstrated its ability to hold me, inch by inch I moved back into the seat and finally touched the back of the seat.

> I FELT SAFE ENOUGH TO ENJOY THAT MUCH OF THE EXPERIENCE

Recognizing that it continued to hold me, I gently began to lean back until I realized that the back of the seat would support me as well. Finally, I looked out over the lake and enjoyed the beautiful scenery. I felt safe enough to enjoy that much of the experience, but it would take me quite a bit longer to test more of the strength of the swing, the chains and the branch before I could feel completely safe on it. Once confident in its safety, it could lend itself to feelings of security, and eventually an ability to swing freely and uninhibited—just like I did as a second grader with someone giving me underdogs.

Just as dolphins freely trust God to provide the air they breathe, my trust in God's care for me grows as I experience more and more of His faithfulness and provision.

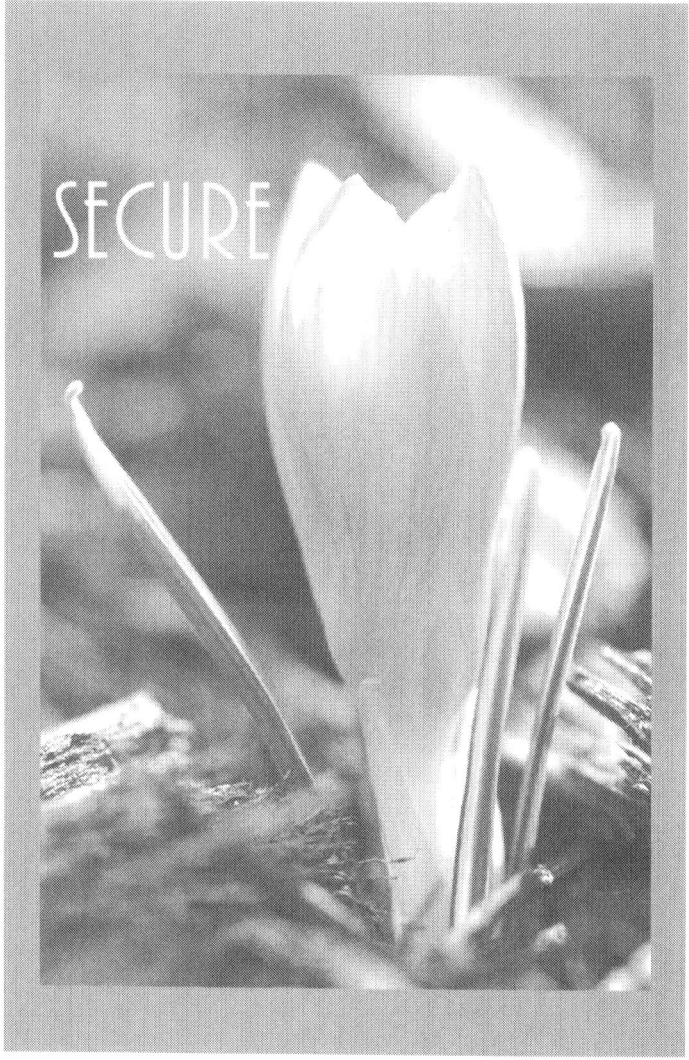

SECURE

se·cure
[səˈkyo͝or]

ADJECTIVE
1.   fixed or fastened so as not to give way, become loose, or be lost.

2.2   feeling confident and free from fear or anxiety.

2.3   feeling no doubts about attaining.

9

AN INSECURE FORTRESS

"Don't worry about anything; instead,
pray about everything. Tell God what you
need, and thank him for all he has done."
–Philippians 4.6, NLT

*I*n Larry Crabb's book, *Inside Out*, he says,

The demand to keep ourselves safe is strong. We look in all the wrong places for the relief our soul desires so badly, developing a style of relating designed to protect ourselves from the pain we fear. Although our self-protective strategies are foolish (even when we get the safety we want, we realize it's not what we want), we still cling to our "right" to protect ourselves. We demand that our pain be relieved. That core demand must be faced before we'll give it up through repentance and learn to re-direct our energy into love.

We so often look to people to redeem us and make us feel safe—the boyfriend or spouse to be the father that didn't do his job, or a friend to be the mother that didn't love us well. So we look to a person to fill a void. God may want to father or mother us (as we should have been fathered or mothered) through someone else of His choice, but it will only fill us if we're seeking God rather than the person.

People CANNOT redeem us. God redeems us when we trust Him with our relationships. God's intent for us in relationship is that we lay down our lives for each other rather than searching for what will fill us. We get it backwards. God blesses us in relationship (and even makes us feel good in many relationships) when we lay down our lives for the other person.

GRAVITY

Just as gravity pulls us down physically, we live in a world where we are constantly being pulled down spiritually as well. We are all being pulled down by life, and we are all in need of being lifted up. Because of that nature, we typically both give and take in relationship. When we are very wounded, though, oftentimes our tendency is to take much more than we give, depleting more people. Some people strongly desire to and can lift us up to some extent, but Jesus understood that to be adequately lifted up, in His physical form, He had to keep going to God, His Father, and spending time with Him.

It's why He often went away from the crowds and His friends in order to be with God. Everything and everyone in this world will be insufficient in lifting us to the place God desires for us to be.

That said, God does desire for us to support each other and help to build each other up by encouraging each other (and in order to encourage others, we have to receive it first from God). Since we are constantly being dragged down, it's important to be intentional about being raised up with God's words to us. Once we are, then we will be able to raise each other up with His words and with sharing what He's doing in our lives. We also lift each other up by sharing what He's speaking to us and with how He's showing Himself faithful and revealing the fruit of His spirit to us (love, joy, peace, patience, kindness, goodness, faithfulness, gentleness and self-control). It's a beautiful interaction when our needs are first met by God. Then our interactions with each other are a strong encouragement and delightful refreshment.

When I was wrestling with feeling a need for support, companionship, connection and understanding, this is what I sensed God speaking to me:

I AM that for you, and I provide it through various means—sometimes people, but not always. I want you to be dependent on ME, not that person. Sometimes I'll provide other things or creatures or circumstances—but not always the same things so you'll know that it's not them but rather ME in them that's meeting your need. That's where you'll find true security. I AM YOUR PEACE."

IT'S NOT THEM
BUT RATHER ME IN THEM
THAT'S MEETING YOUR NEED

I hate feelings of insecurity. "Insecure" defined is:
— adj
1. anxious or afraid; not confident or certain
2. not adequately protected: an insecure fortress
3. unstable or shaky.

It easy to gravitate toward people or things to help us feel secure. We often want something to fill those voids in us. Until we learn to be content without the things we want, we won't truly be content WITH the things we want. But when we learn to be content without, we end up finding something of even greater value than the things we want—peace.

God offers help for my insecurity when He says in Philippians 4.6-7 (interpretation added based on definition):
Do not be anxious [insecure] about anything, but in every situation, by prayer and petition, with thanksgiving, present your requests to God. And the peace of God, which transcends all

understanding, will guard your hearts and your minds in Christ Jesus.

Another version (NLT) says:

Don't worry [be insecure] about anything; instead, pray about everything. Tell God what you need, and thank him for all he has done. Then you will experience God's peace, which exceeds anything we can understand. His peace will guard your hearts and minds as you live in Christ Jesus.

Just a few verses later, Paul goes on to say:

I know what it is to be in need, and I know what it is to have plenty. I have learned the secret of being content in any and every situation, whether well fed or hungry, whether living in plenty or in want. (Philippians 4.12)

May we have that kind of peace as we give God our needs (and trust Him with them), and as we remember what He's done for us already so we're able to live above feelings of insecurity.

10

ABLE TO CALM YOUR FEARS

"For the Lord your God is living among
you. He is a mighty savior. He will take
delight in you with gladness. With his love,
he will calm all your fears. He will rejoice
over you with joyful songs."
–Zephaniah 3.17, NLT

God is living among us. Sometimes I forget that. I mean, I know it in my head, but then I go about my daily activities as if He's far away. But He's not—He is right here with you and me—able to calm our fears (give peace where we feel anxiety, provide order in our chaos, relieve our stress) with His love. Over and over I hear His gentle reminders of Psalm 46.10a where "He says, 'Be still and know that I am God.'" When I choose to be still, I'm in a good position to receive His love so that He is able to quiet me in it.

Another version of Zephaniah 3.17 says, "...he will rest in his love; he will joy over thee with singing...."

(ASV) When I imagine God at rest with me, it actually makes me think of my grandma. When I was young, I would spend the night at her house. I remember her tucking me in when I went to bed at night. She would snuggle up next to me and tell me stories and sing songs to me. It calmed me. She was at rest with me in her love for me. Thinking back on that still brings me a sense of calmness.

EMBRACE

Sometimes our wounded hearts can't speak or even receive words. Instead, our hearts may simply need to be still, rest peacefully and experience the comfort of a safe, nurturing embrace where words are not necessary.

The song, "I Lift My Hands" by Chris Tomlin has been speaking to me.

"Be still, there is a healer
His love is deeper than the sea
His mercy, it is unfailing
His arms, a fortress for the weak."

As we turn toward God's arms to be our fortress, especially when we are weak, we will find a place where our hearts can be still.

ABLE TO CALM YOUR FEARS | 75

SAFE AT 30,000 FEET

When I'm at home, I lock my doors at night. I watch over fires that I have in my fireplace. I make sure the burners on the gas stove are all turned off before I go to bed, and I clean the lint trap in the dryer before every use. I even wear my seatbelt when I'm driving. I do a lot of things to help ensure my (and my family's) physical safety.

I fly a fair amount, and one day I was flying somewhere and there was a lot of turbulence. I wear my seatbelt in the plane because they tell me to, but I really don't think it's going to do a whole lot of good if I fall from 30,000 feet along with a whole lot of other bodies and tons of metal crashing into me—although I've never tried it. With the turbulence, I started thinking about how little control I had over my physical safety at that point. I looked around at other people—the handful that I could see. Some looked to be sleeping. Some looked nervous. No one was panicking, although some were very wide-eyed and attentive to the random jerky motion of the plane. I was mostly just curious.

One time, Jesus was asleep in a boat while His disciples feared for their lives as wild winds and a storm violently thrashed them. There were other boats with them—I imagine those in the other boats were probably fearful as well, although Scripture doesn't say. But while they were in the boat on their way to "the other side", it says...

A furious squall came up, and the waves broke over the boat, so that it was nearly swamped. Jesus was in the stern, sleeping on a cushion. The disciples woke him and said to him, "Teacher, don't you care if we drown?"

He got up, rebuked the wind and said to the waves, "Quiet! Be still!" Then the wind died down and it was completely calm.

He said to his disciples, "Why are you so afraid? Do you still have no faith?" (Mark 4.37-40)

How does someone sleep so peacefully when the winds are wild, when storms in our lives thrash us, and when turbulence in our circumstances and relationships leaves us hopeless? How do you sleep peacefully when a diagnosis is cancer or when your spouse wants a divorce? How do you sleep peacefully when your child disowns you, or the pregnancy test is still negative after years of trying to start a family? How do you sleep peacefully when your greatest fears are occurring in your life?

We have all kinds storms and turbulence in our lives: physical storms, emotional storms, relational storms and even spiritual storms. Regardless of the storm, He seems to be reminding them (and us) that He has power over all things. I wonder what kind of response He wanted from them. Their response indicated that they were convinced they were all going to drown and thought He should be aware, maybe so He could panic with them.

I wonder if the response He hoped for would have been something like:

> Jesus, the storm is really beating us up, and it's more than we can handle. We know You have the power to do something about it—whether it's stopping the storm, shielding us from it, or giving us the ability to swim in it if needed. You said, "Everyone who calls on the name of the Lord will be saved." (Romans 10.13) We need to be saved; and we know You have that power.

He was so patient with them, saving them even before they had faith in Him. But His desire was for them to trust that He would take care of them.

NOT THE LIFE I WANTED

I went through a season of several years where I lamented that things were not as I had wanted. My life wasn't turning out like I had dreamed and hoped.

Many biblical accounts reveal the same thing. Sarah believed she would bear children and be the mother of many nations. But she grew old and cynical, and she began believing that her dream was thwarted. The life she was living was not the life that she had wanted, and she gave up hope.

Joseph saw a vision of himself living a powerful life, but then he was sold into slavery, falsely accused and spent many years in prison—probably not the life he had wanted.

So many others:

- Mary was privileged to be chosen to give birth to the Son of God, but then had to witness the torturous death of her son—certainly not the life she had wanted.

- John the Baptist was called to prepare the way for Jesus, but was then put in prison and beheaded.

- Leah no doubt had dreamed of having a husband who adored her. Instead she was given to Jacob, but she wasn't his choice.

- Jacob was in love with Rachel, and he worked for several years to have the privilege of marrying her. Instead, he was given her sister, Leah. Not the life he had wanted.

- Hagar was mistreated and oppressed by Sarah who lorded authority over her—not the life she had wanted.

- Job, of course, built an amazing empire only to see it all collapse in a day—not the life he had wanted.

But what did all these people have in common? Although at times their faith wavered, they didn't let go of God.

ALTHOUGH AT TIMES THEIR FAITH WAVERED, THEY DIDN'T LET GO OF GOD

God fulfilled HIS dream and purpose for their lives. In some cases their purpose was fulfilled, although maybe the dream wasn't fulfilled until they stood in His presence. It was certainly fulfilled then.

- Sarah became the mother of many nations, but only in a way that God could accomplish it.
- Joseph became a faithful and powerful leader that could only preserve the country and the people because of what God accomplished in him through many years earlier.
- Mary saw her son raised from the dead, and His death and resurrection accomplishing God's amazing purpose.
- Jacob eventually married Rachel.
- Hagar was seen by, pursued by and stood face to face with God.
- Job received ten times what he had lost.

But more importantly, each one finished with a deeper faith, a closer and more intimate relationship with God, and a more firm commitment to Him and His plan and purpose for them, despite God's ways and understanding being beyond their comprehension.

They all ended with a different life than they had wanted, but a perspective that found peace and comfort in their purpose.

11

DELIGHTING HIS HEART

"... the Lord delights in those who fear
him, who put their hope in his unfailing
love."
–Psalm 147.11

o you ever feel pressure to do the "right"
things to please God? I'm thinking about the
things that will last into eternity. If "faith,
hope and love" are the things that God says will remain (I
Corinthians 13.13), then it seems that what's pleasing to
Him has more to do with our heart than our
performance. So then I'm prompted to ask myself:

- "Is my heart believing what He says—truth from
  His Word?"
- "Do I give up or do I persevere with a confident
  heart as I look ahead to a future sculpted by
  God?"

- "Is my heart embracing His love for me and allowing that love to overflow into everyone that my life touches?"

These are the things that will last and be a sweet aroma to Him. These things delight His heart.

POWERLESS

Much of my life I felt pressure to do what pleases others before I even considered if it was God's intention. I learned that it was in those times that I let something besides God direct me that I ended up feeling powerless in life and controlled. When something felt out of my control, or if I felt controlled, as in I didn't have a choice to speak of, or I felt coerced, I would feel much tension. Something in me knew that I wasn't designed to respond that way. God designed me to choose to align with His intentions for me. He doesn't force me, but He does know what's best for me and pursues me to lead me in the best direction for my life. In that, though, He gives me power to choose. Regardless of my choices, He's always drawing me to His heart. And I am drawn to His heart. Because of that, He's able to help me see when I get off track. And sometimes I do get off track.

Lord, I haven't worshiped You like You deserve to be worshiped. I haven't loved You as You deserve to be loved. I haven't loved my husband as You designed a wife to love her husband. I haven't loved my family, my kids, my household as You designed each of them to be loved.

Continue to work in me to heal me, to grow me, to free me of my selfishness, so that I can love as You designed me to love. In the meantime, thank You for Your kindness that leads me to repentance, for Your patience as I slowly continue to move toward You and Your ways, and for Your grace that not only covers over my shortcomings but allows You to see the covering of Christ when You look at me. Thank you for Your grace that actually strips away every sin, every imperfection, every broken part of me, everything I've used to help myself feel intact, everything that is not of You and Your beauty. Thank you that Your grace allows You to see me as the person You created me to be... just as You created me... with every detailed perfection that only You could design. Because of Your grace that covers me, You see me as I was meant to be... a creation that You stand in awe of simply because You are the designer. And it's Your grace that allows me to experience an amazing love that lets me forget that I'm flawed.

YOU DON'T HAVE TO DO ANYTHING

Sometimes tension rises in me pretty high before I recognize that something is wrong. I start taking on more and more responsibility, more and more tasks, more and more that others request of me—all good stuff—until I'm overwhelmed and want to quit everything. One time when this happened, I was talking to God about it and sensed Him speaking to me: "You don't have to do anything."

It was a jaw-dropping moment as I realized I'm killing myself to do all these things, much like how Martha may have been feeling when she complained about Mary not helping her. Yet God was reminding me that life is more simple than I sometimes make it. "You don't have to do anything." He would love me the same whether I'm doing everything, or letting everything go.

What happened was that I felt free—free to do nothing, and freed up to do whatever I wanted as I aligned with Him. Suddenly, I had renewed energy and motivation. Typically, when He's given me this reminder (which has been many times!), the things I'm doing actually tend to change very little, but my whole outlook changes dramatically.

The pressure, in those times, turns to joy, maybe because I'm given freedom to choose. And because I love the freedom, care and grace that He provides for me, I want to give to and serve Him all the more. Maybe also because I know He's already pleased with me, so there's no pressure to perform. If I feel like I have to perform for Him to be pleased with me, my actions are fear-based. When I serve Him knowing that He is already pleased with me, and I don't HAVE to do anything, my actions are love-based.

12

GOD FALLS HEAD OVER HEELS
IN LOVE WITH DUST

"As a father has compassion on his children,
so the Lord has compassion on those who fear him;
for he knows how we are formed,
he remembers that we are dust.
… But from everlasting to everlasting
the Lord's love is with those who fear him…."
–Psalm 103:13-14, 17a

*W*e are just dust. Let that sink in. I dust things in my house and want to get rid of the dust, and yet you and I are dust that breathes. We are dust that has a heartbeat. We are dust that has been transformed into amazing and intricate detail. We are dust with purpose. Dust that, at God's command, has taken on the temporary form of blood and bone and muscle. And then, with the magnificent work that goes into transforming dust into something beautiful and alive, God delights in His work and falls in love with it—head over heels in love.

With that in mind, listen to how He describes His love for people made of dust:

"For God so loved the world that he gave his one and only Son, that whoever believes in him shall not perish but have eternal life." (John 3.16)

"But because of his great love for us, God, who is rich in mercy, made us alive with Christ even when we were dead in transgressions—it is by grace you have been saved. And God raised us up with Christ and seated us with him in the heavenly realms in Christ Jesus, ..." (Ephesians 2.4-6)

"'For I know the plans I have for you,' declares the Lord, 'plans to prosper you and not to harm you, plans to give you hope and a future.'" (Jeremiah 29.11)

"God saw all that he had made, and it was very good." (Genesis 1.31a)

"For God, who said, 'Let light shine out of darkness,' made his light shine in our hearts to give us the light of the knowledge of God's glory displayed in the face of Christ." (2 Corinthians 4.6)

"Christ Jesus who died—more than that, who was raised to life—is at the right hand of God and is also interceding for us. Who shall separate us from the love of Christ? Shall trouble or hardship or persecution or famine or nakedness or danger or sword? As it is written:

'For your sake we face death all day long;
   we are considered as sheep to be slaughtered.'

No, in all these things we are more than conquerors through him who loved us." (Romans 8.34b-37)

"But you are a chosen people, a royal priesthood, a holy nation, God's special possession, that you may declare the praises of him who called you out of darkness into his wonderful light." (1 Peter 2.9)

"You did not choose me, but I chose you and appointed you so that you might go and bear fruit—fruit that will last—and so that whatever you ask in my name the Father will give you." (John 15.16)

"For you created my inmost being;
   you knit me together in my mother's womb.

I praise you because I am fearfully and wonderfully made ...." (Psalm 139.13-14)

"How precious to me are your thoughts, God!
   How vast is the sum of them!
Were I to count them,
   they would outnumber the grains of sand—"
(Psalm 139.17-18a)

"You can tell for sure that you are now fully adopted as his own children because God sent the Spirit of his Son into our lives crying out, 'Papa! Father!' Doesn't that privilege of intimate conversation with God make it plain that you are not a slave, but a child? And if you are a child, you're also an heir, with complete access to the inheritance." (Galatians 4.6-7, MSG)

"'Do not be afraid, little flock, for your Father has been pleased to give you the kingdom.'" (Luke 12.32)

"…as a bridegroom rejoices over his bride,
    so will your God rejoice over you." (Isaiah 62.5)

"'The Lord your God is with you,
    the Mighty Warrior who saves.
He will take great delight in you;
    in his love he will no longer rebuke you,
    but will rejoice over you with singing.'" (Zephaniah 3.17)

"He will redeem them from oppression and violence, for their lives are precious to him." (Psalm 72.14, NLT)

"'Anyone who harms you harms my most precious possession.'" (Zechariah 2.8b, NLT)

"I will come back and take you to be with me that you also may be where I am." (John 14.3b)

"I will… give you a heart of flesh." (Ezekiel 36.26)

And God spoke to my heart: "I gave you a soft heart so I could lay my head on your heart."

13

FALLING BRANCHES

"I will remove from them their heart of
stone and give them a heart of flesh."
–Ezekiel 11.19b

I had stopped at a park and a large tree got my
attention. I was drawn to it, so I parked right
in front of it and took a picture of it (p. 91). It
was obviously rotting and falling apart. Then I started
talking to God.

I'm distraught and overwhelmed. Something
very uncomfortable is stirring in me—anxiety that
is much bigger than my circumstances.

There are people in my life who are not living
as they should. I want to talk to them, but I'm
afraid to approach them because I don't think
they're teachable or open to correction. I love
when they're engaged with me and talkative—it
delights my heart. But right now they're
disengaged and isolating; something about that

bothers me and I "feel like" I need to fix it...and quickly.

Then I listened for God...

Notice the tree in front of you. Where there is rotting on the inside, there is brokenness. And where there is brokenness, branches fall. Where branches fall, those close by can be hurt.

These people have something rotting on the inside.

What's rotting inside is how they see themselves. And that brokenness—and falling apart—impacts those close to them.

I got some good thoughts from my husband too. He noted that it didn't seem that my desire was about correction, but more about asking them if they want to be healthy and move toward Christ. And then assuming they do, then I'm able to give suggestions for how to do that—offering ideas and insight into things they can do to achieve their own desires/goals.

That was helpful. I still wanted to look at why I didn't feel peaceful when they were disengaged and isolating—with "falling branches" of brokenness. I believed I should be able to separate myself from their stuff and maintain my own peace, but I needed God's insight.

I sensed God speaking to me through Psalm 27.14,
"Wait for the Lord;

> be strong and take heart
> and wait for the Lord."

I find that I often want to run ahead of Him and make things work out as they "should", mostly because I'm uncomfortable when circumstances aren't the way they should be. I'm learning more and more, though, to rest in knowing He's tending to the circumstances. He's patient with the process it takes for us to become more like Him and reflect His character. He knows that it typically takes a whole lot of behind-the-scenes work to transform us in a way that is permanent. So I listen to His gentle reminders, and with a heart that has confidence in Him, I try to focus on leaning on Him to give me strength to wait for Him.

As for my discomfort in the waiting, God reminded me that He has transformed my

A HEART OF FLESH IS TENDER AND VULNERABLE

heart from a heart of stone to a heart of flesh. A heart of flesh is tender and vulnerable, feeling more deeply (just as He does) the impact of imperfect relationships. The following devotional from the National Association for Christian Recovery (NACR) gave me courage.

"I will remove from them their heart of stone and give them a heart of flesh." (Ezekiel 11:19)

God promises us a heart transplant. God promises to change us. Our stone hearts will be removed and in their place will be put a heart of flesh.

A heart of stone is a dead heart. It is closed to honest, intimate relationships. A heart of stone is unmerciful with itself and with others. But we do become attached to our hearts of stone. And we find ourselves fearing God's promised transplant. Our stone hearts have one thing in their favor— they allow us to feel strong and to appear strong to others. A stone heart is a protected heart. It seems invulnerable. You cannot wound a heart of stone.

God's offer of a heart transplant is a promise of life. A heart of flesh is alive. Only a flesh heart can feel joy. Only a flesh heart can celebrate. Only a heart of flesh can give and receive love. But, the vulnerability of a heart of flesh scares us. A flesh heart does not seem as well protected as a heart of stone. It can feel joy, but it can also feel pain. You can wound a heart of flesh.

God promises to change us. God will remove our hearts of stone and give us hearts of flesh.

> I like the safety of my stone heart, Lord.
> But it is hard, cold, dead.
> It is a heartless heart, bloodless, lifeless.
> Remove it from me.
> I want a heart of flesh, Lord.
> I want life.
> But I am afraid.
> Give me the courage to say "yes"
> to your promise of life today.
> Remove my heart of stone and
> give me a heart of flesh.
> Amen.

(Copyright Dale and Juanita Ryan)

With my heart of flesh, navigating relationships can sometimes be painful. I don't like discord and tension in relationships. I suppose most people don't.

I remember several years ago when two friends were in conflict at my house. I was not at peace and wanted it resolved. But I remember God clearly speaking to me, "It's okay for them to be a mess."

God began giving me more and more peace in those kinds of situations as He showed me how He works in the messiness. Stopping a conflict might make the circumstances more peaceful in the short term, but allowing messiness for a time allows opportunity for them to work through it to get to transformation.

14

SECOND DESIRES

"The boundary lines have fallen for me in
pleasant places; surely I have a delightful
inheritance."
–Psalm 16.6

My friend had strict boundaries. I didn't like it at the time; in fact, it felt excruciating. We had a time to meet once every two weeks. I looked forward to those times, but in between those times, I would often feel insecure. I wanted reassurance (that was my first desire), and I felt that a lack of connection would result in relational distance—and that was scary for me. When I would try to call or text or email her, she wouldn't respond. I don't know for sure why, but I do know that God used it for good in my life.

My second (and greater) desire was to feel secure and free. In the long run, her boundaries helped me, but it helped me because she ALWAYS delighted in me when I did see her. Others prior to her had had boundaries, but their boundaries were not necessarily combined with the same level of delight in me. I needed the boundaries along with the consistent peace, delight and love that gave me security. It was THEN that I learned that relational distance could be safe and secure. As a result, I began to feel free, and my second and greater desire was fulfilled.

"NOTHING TASTES AS GOOD AS THIN FEELS"

When I first heard this saying, it felt motivating. I loved the way I felt when I was in good shape, and it helped motivate me to say no to the things that didn't support the goal of being thin.

Truth be told, though, I still had the desire for the things that didn't support the goal. Actually, both things were desires, and sometimes the first desire to come along (in this case, the food temptation) won out over the second desire (the desire to be thin, in shape and feel good).

For the past several years, I've been pursuing a healthier lifestyle than I ever had before. My motivation in this is to do all I can to be free of disease and have the ability to move well so I can enjoy life to the fullest. So I exercise regularly, get enough sleep, drink half my weight in ounces of filtered water every day. I incorporate superfoods into my meals; I eat healthy fats and stay away from unhealthy fats. I eat healthy meat but I limit my intake of it. I stay away from white flour and sugar, and I substitute with gluten free flour and grains and use pure maple syrup, dates, monk fruit extract, coconut sugar and stevia as sweeteners. I eat foods that will keep my body more alkaline than acidic, I eat organic non-GMO foods as much as possible, and I stay away from processed foods.

I didn't make all these changes overnight; I've taken baby steps to incorporate them into my life. Oftentimes, I just look for things I can change that help me to feel better. When I would wake up every morning with aching joints, I wanted to find a way to reduce the achiness. I experimented and found that when I significantly reduced sugar in my diet, the joint aches went away. I like that. Not having achy joints was a strong desire, but it was a second desire. I had to delay the first desire of fleeting gratification that I could have with sugar in order to have the longer lasting second desire of feeling good.

NEW ORLEANS

New Orleans is one of my favorite places to visit. My husband and I have been there several times. We stay in the peaceful Garden District. We enjoy going for walks and admiring the impressive old houses, huge sprawling trees and above-ground cemeteries. Our hotel is right on the St. Charles street car line, so we can just walk out the front door of the hotel and jump on the street car that will take us into the French Quarter to enjoy street music, intriguing artwork, a view of the Mississippi River and its steam boats, the sounds of jazz bands in restaurants and delightful food.

Recently, we took our friends who had never been there before. We stepped up the pace and packed in as much as we could to allow them to experience all the things we enjoy about New Orleans, including plantation and swamp tours.

We spent a lot of time walking, so I was happy that I got that kind of exercise in. But when it came to food, the first day I ate great-tasting healthy food and felt great afterward. Then the others were interested in trying more of the culturally authentic food. One thing I understand about myself is that when temptation is in front of me, I have a hard time saying no.

For instance, when I'm in Trader Joe's and the Tiramisu is calling out to me from the freezer section as it always does, I've found that it's easier to say no to it when it's in the store freezer than when it's in my freezer at home. (I've learned from that experience.) So now, when I'm walking past the dessert section in Trader Joe's, I look in the opposite direction (setting up a boundary) because I want to have my long-term second desire more than the strong short-term fleeting first desire.

Back to New Orleans, though. For the next three days, I gave in to first desires and ate gluten, white flour, unhealthy fats, carbs and sugar (in the forms of white rice, sausage, beignets, bread pudding, crème brûlée and even a taste of fried alligator). And all that without any of the healthier things I would normally eat. Basically, I ate like the majority of people.

What I noticed, though, was that after just two days of eating that way, I felt heavy, bloated, lethargic, had trouble sleeping and my joints were aching. I knew I needed to make changes. When we got home, I immediately got back on track, pursued my second desires, and within two days I was feeling better again.

The principle of first desires and second desires, of course, can be applied to any area of our lives—and imagine the transformation that we could experience if we did apply it to every area of our lives. We would have productive days. We would be able to experience deep intimacy with God. We would thrive in so many beautiful ways.

15

GARBAGE TRUCKS

"Jesus said, 'Father, forgive them, for
they do not know what they are doing.'"
–Luke 23.34

As I'm writing this, it's winter here in Michigan. We've had a lot of snow, and the roads are a mess, making driving a bit challenging at times.

The other day, my friend Robbie was driving in her car. In the lane to the left of her was a garbage truck. At one point, the driver began moving into her lane and pushing her off the road, but also made contact with the driver's side of her car and scraped the whole side and damaged the front quarter panel before continuing to drive off, seemingly, completely unaware. The garbage truck did a lot of damage to her car, but the garbage truck driver seemed to have no idea.

People hurt us. They do things that cause damage to our lives, and sometimes a whole a lot of expense; and they may have absolutely no idea.

A friend doesn't keep me in the loop on important communication.

I'm bothered and hurt when someone communicates with me in a way that feels harsh.

Another person forgets to let me know if he won't be home for dinner when I planned a nice family dinner together.

Another isn't home when it's his turn to shovel the driveway that is snow covered when I need to go somewhere (and my back aches from all the times I've already shoveled).

Another stays up too late and can't be ready on time in the morning when we have to go somewhere.

One friend was supposed to pay me for something and has probably forgotten.

I'm wounded and they have no idea. The thing is, they are pursuing what they believe is good and right for them to do, and they don't even know the impact they're having on me or others because they may be, figuratively, driving a garbage truck. Their intentions are good; they just don't always know the impact of some of the things they're doing.

There are other times when people do things that wrongfully hurt us, but they think their actions are acceptable. I'm thinking of the man who texted my friend to tell her they're relationally not right for each other—a conversation that should take place face to face. Or the person who emailed another friend to discontinue her employment. Maybe it's fear that causes someone to hide behind the written communication that should instead be face to face. Regardless, they don't seem to see the hurtfulness of their impact.

Jesus recognized that very thing as he hung on the cross to cover people's shortcomings and sins. He asked His Father to "'forgive them, for they do not know what they are doing.'" (Luke 23.34) It stands to reason that I'm also probably one who doesn't recognize the negative impact I may have at times—I, too, figuratively drive a garbage truck at times and "don't know what [I'm] doing." I need the Father's forgiveness as well. Knowing that helps me to see others in the same way and forgive them.

VULNERABLE

Ironically, when Jesus said to become like a little child, He had demonstrated that Himself in becoming baby Jesus, vulnerable to the authority of His parents and vulnerable to the dangers of other people.

There are times for us to put boundaries in place with others. There are times for us to speak the truth in love with others. And there are times when we will be accused or blamed, sometimes, seemingly wrongfully. I tend to become weighed down when I experience this. I realize there are times when I can be blind to my wrongfulness. I was talking to God about this and sensed Him speaking this to my heart:

"Others can blame you, but you don't have to receive it. Bring it to Me and we will together hold it under the light of truth."

"OTHERS CAN BLAME YOU, BUT YOU DON'T HAVE TO RECEIVE IT. BRING IT TO ME AND WE WILL TOGETHER HOLD IT UNDER THE LIGHT OF TRUTH."

Somehow, it brought security and freedom and lifted that heavy weight from my shoulders.

DON'T TRY TO CHANGE ME!

Sometimes I'm not very accepting (and sometimes I even attack) when someone tries to make me change or make me see things their way. I can get pretty stubborn...I mean, tenacious. I lived as a people-pleaser for so long, wanting to be accepted. Now my dilemma is still *wanting* to be accepted, but not wanting to be a people-pleaser. It's more important to me to know and live out my convictions, yet it can trigger some deep pain when I'm not accepted because of it.

Jesus wasn't accepted. People tried to change Him, and they even attacked Him, but He knew how to be at peace anyway. He knew how to respond appropriately, and He knew when to keep His mouth shut. I want to live that way.

Sometimes when I'm opposed, depending on the relationship, I may feel fear, frustration or panic, especially when it's a closer relationship (although I still have no interest in debating issues). One day a close friend opposed my thinking, which I was usually okay with, but this particular day she pointed out something in me that needed correction, and she was right. It, however, stirred up fear, frustration AND panic, all at the same time.

Later I recognized that I held the belief that I'm not accepted when I'm opposed.

> I HELD THE BELIEF THAT I'M NOT ACCEPTED WHEN I'M OPPOSED

Interestingly, that belief didn't hold up to what I believed was true about her. As I contemplated other situations where I felt opposition and unacceptance, I began to see that some people actually thrive on debate and get energized by it (which sounds crazy to me, but I know it's true). And in those times when they seem to oppose me, there's typically, actually, no unacceptance in their opposition, but it's more just a love for debate and trying to resolve truth.

There are occasional times when that person really is unaccepting, but not always—maybe not even most of the time.

WHAT DO YOU HEAR?

What determines the way you hear God? Is the God you're listening to the God of the Bible or the god you learned from distorted teaching and imperfect examples?

When I really thought about those questions, I realized that my perceptions were swayed by imperfect (and sometimes harmful) leaders who had impacted my life. One pastor refused to get involved when another leader in the church was emotionally unstable and had been emotionally abusing and condemning me and others in the church. Another pastor refused to look into my own sexual abuse situation because I was an adult by the time it was known. Yet another leader was kind but insisted on things being done his way. Then there was another who micromanaged; another who looked down on anyone who wasn't in full time ministry; and still another who was uninvolved and completely uninterested in what I was doing in ministry.

I asked myself more questions that were discussed in a radio teaching:

- Do you hear from God as a loving father or a demanding father?
- Is he intimate or distant?
- Is he patient and understanding and willing to teach through failure, or is he impatient and condemning and intolerant? (Maybe harshly questioning, "Why haven't you learned yet?")
- Is he gentle or strict?

I could see that I was swayed by my experiences. I knew God was loving and kind, but I also projected onto Him some of the shortcomings of some of my leaders. Because of it, I saw Him as a bit demanding and expecting me to do whatever *He* wanted, even if it was under compulsion. Of course, when I did, I was doing it out of guilt and obligation rather than joy, gratitude and love.

As I processed these thoughts with Him, I, again, lovingly heard Him say, "You don't have to do anything." It surprised me, but I understood. I'm His child, and He will love me regardless of what I do. He will love me if I do what He has planned for me to do, and He will love me if I don't. It's unconditional. He cannot NOT love me because He IS love. And His desire, above everything else, is for me to love: "If I give all I possess to the poor and give over my body to hardship that I may boast, but do not have love, I gain nothing." (1 Corinthians 13.3)

I began to pay attention to when I was hearing Him as a demanding Father rather than a loving Father. And when I was hearing Him as distant rather than intimate; or strict rather than gentle. I began to recognize when I heard Him as impatient, condemning and intolerant rather than patient, understanding and willing to gently teach me through failure.

As a result, my relationship with Him grew in intimacy, beauty and desire.

HIS PLAN FOR REDEMPTION

In the midst of learning this, I was wrestling with a decision. Someone needed a stable place to live for a little while, and I sensed God leading us to provide just such a place, but knowing some of their story, I was very hesitant. I felt like I had to say yes to God, but I knew if I did at that point, it would be under compulsion.

So I cried; and I cried out to God. I had a lot of legitimate reasons to say no; but I still sensed God's gentle nudge. As I continued to wrestle and cry, I sensed Him nudging me AND simultaneously giving me freedom as I heard, "You don't HAVE to do anything." I knew He would love me and accept me regardless of my choice.

But then I continued to hear Him speak to my heart:

> Let me bless you.
>
> You've learned what I've taught you about "Father forgive them for they know not what they do." When you pray this, you're asking Me to not even remember their sin—to treat them as if they didn't even commit a sin.

I responded:

Yes, I've talked about how I can pray that regarding someone who sexually abused me, because I don't want him to be punished for his wrong choices, but rather I want to see him living in wholeness with You. My heart is that he would know Your love and Your plan for his life and walk in that plan.

SELF-PROTECTION…
ISN'T NECESSARILY
A PATH TO FREEDOM

I sensed God's reply:

Now you have an opportunity to live this out regarding someone else who made some poor choices.

My plan is not necessarily safe, but it is always sovereign.

My plan is that the truth would set you free, but freedom in the truest sense is not necessarily physical. Self-protection, in an attempt to keep potential danger at bay, isn't necessarily a path to freedom.

A POW or a prisoner in a Nazi concentration camp certainly wants physical freedom, but Corrie ten Boom could attest that yes, the body longs for physical freedom, but emotional and spiritual freedom provide the deepest peace:

"Forgiveness is setting the prisoner free, only to find out that the prisoner was me."

–Corrie ten Boom

Think of the many long-time prisoners who are released and end up committing suicide. They received physical freedom but lacked emotional and spiritual freedom.

"We must mirror God's love in the midst of a world full of hatred. We are the mirrors of God's love, so we may show Jesus by our lives."
–Corrie ten Boom

16

A ROCK & A HARD PLACE

> "'I am the LORD, the God of all mankind. Is
> anything too hard for me?'"
> –Jeremiah 32.27

My friend S. Kristi Douglas wrote this on Facebook:

I was praying this morning about a situation that has frustrated me for quite some time. Not seeing any resolution, I prayed, "I feel like I'm stuck between a rock and a hard place." Then the Holy Spirit brought a Scripture to my mind. While in trouble, King David prayed, "From the end of the earth I will cry to You, when my heart is overwhelmed; lead me to THE ROCK that is higher than I." (Psalm 61:2, NKJV *emphasis added*) Who is THE ROCK? It is Christ of course! So what about that hard place? God Himself answers back, "'I am the LORD, the God of all mankind. Is anything TOO

HARD for me?'" (Jeremiah 32:27, *emphasis added*). So, today, I've determined that even though I don't yet have the answer, I'll just sit still. Because being between a rock and hard place may not be such a bad place to be after all.

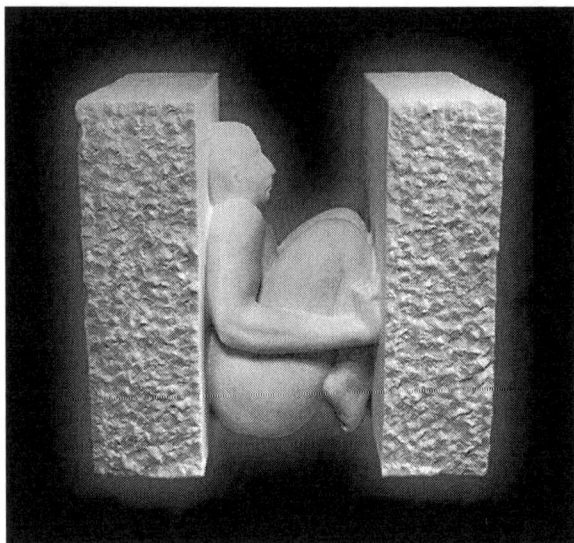

IMPOSSIBLE PLACES

Many years ago, God was deepening my faith. He had taken me through a challenging time, but to be honest, I think I could have gotten through it without Him. The reality was, it wasn't anything impossible to get through, just challenging. I can get through a lot of challenging things on my own. But the reality is, God still wants to lead us through those challenging things we can do on our own.

He brought to mind how He called Peter to walk to Him on the water. What He spoke to me was this:

I've had you in a boat on the beach, practicing getting in and out of the boat on the sandy beach. Now I'm pushing your boat out into the water, and I'm calling you into the realm of impossibility.

SUDDENLY, I COULD SEE THE SIGNIFICANCE OF RELYING ON HIM IN THE SMALLER THINGS

Suddenly, I could see the significance of relying on Him in the smaller (possible) things, because now relying on Him was becoming a matter of success and failure—maybe even life and death. If I wasn't relying on Him now, whatever I faced wasn't going to happen.

Fortunately, I know Him to be patient and gracious, just like He was with Peter. He called Peter to the privilege of doing the impossible. If I fail, He will catch me, but I'd really like to keep my eyes on Him and make it all the way to Him, delightfully smiling as I do the impossible.

17

LEAN ON ME AND STAND TALL

"Yes, everything else is worthless when
compared with the infinite value of
knowing Christ Jesus my Lord."
–Philippians 3.8a, NLT

A conversation with God...

Me: I'm going through a time of changes, and it's scary. Sometimes I don't know if I can do it—or even what it is that I really need to do. I just know it's scary and unsettling much of the time.

God: You can do all things through Me. I will empower you to do whatever I call you to do. I will give you words when you need them, and as you lean on Me and keep communicating with Me about it, I will lead you in each step to take.

Me: I guess I just like the security of knowing what's ahead and the steps it'll take to accomplish this phase. I suppose that's walking by sight and not by faith—like You're calling me to walk by. Walking by sight is being in control myself, whereas walking by faith—not necessarily knowing the next move—is trusting Your control and sovereignty and goodness.

God: Yes, that's it. Just as my Son didn't have an easy road to travel, your road will also have high winds at times, potholes, careless drivers and dangerous curves, but I promise to hold onto you, and I will never let you go.

DISCIPLINE AND GUIDANCE

I tend to think of discipline negatively, like forceful actions or harsh words. I'm recognizing that discipline is simply correction to go the right way. It should provide safety, security and freedom.

> DISCIPLINE IS SIMPLY CORRECTION TO GO THE RIGHT WAY

Proverbs 12.1 says, "Whoever loves discipline loves knowledge, but whoever hates correction is stupid."

That does make me wonder about my youth when I did not appreciate discipline... I suppose I was learning to not be stupid. Nonetheless, I can see that discipline is guidance in the right direction. It helps to move us in the direction we should go.

An example I thought of was a horse and buggy. The horse is given a harness to help the driver guide him. The horse is given blinders to prevent distraction that might take him off course or allow him to succumb to fear. The good and godly driver knows their perfect destination and how to get there. The driver knows where they need to go, and it would be "stupid" for the horse to hate the guidance invoked to get him there. The driver tugs gently on the reins to move in a direction toward their destination. Likewise, God gently tugs on the reins of our lives to guide us in the right direction—the direction that allows us to run and live out our purpose in the way that He created us to passionately live it out.

JESUS AND MY SPINE

My chiropractor, whom I loved and saw regularly for nine years, passed away a few months ago. I was seeing him for maintenance every four weeks. As long as I stayed on that schedule, I was pretty stable—without headaches, shoulder pain and sciatica issues. After his death, I'd been planning to start seeing someone else with whom I'm familiar, but I kept putting it off. Lately, I've been struggling more and more with all kinds of aches—most of them focused on my right side—headaches, neck and shoulder pain, discomfort in my throat, hip discomfort, and even my right foot was troublesome. I was becoming very concerned and decided to make an appointment to see my primary doctor, but it'll be a couple weeks yet before I'm able to see her.

I also decided to go ahead and make an appointment with the new chiropractor. I was able to get in to see her in just two days. That was today, and since I was a new patient, she did x-rays. The x-rays showed the slight fracture in my lower spine that I knew existed—caused from a fall I took trying to ski when I was a teenager. But the x-rays also showed that there was a very slight twist in my lower spine as well as in my neck. As she talked about it, explaining that it looks to be a congenital condition, and commented on the possible affects of it over time, things started adding up. My spine being ever-so-slightly out of alignment was wreaking havoc on the rest of my body. Her work on me today helped to get me back to a more stable place, but without maintenance, it will move my body in a wrong direction. It's much like a marksman who takes aim at a target 100 yards away. Once he's perfectly aimed, even moving his aim just a millimeter can cause him to miss his target by several feet.

In the same way, when I am ever-so-slightly out of alignment with God, that misalignment may not show up immediately, but it will evidence itself over time—and sometimes the problems at that point are very difficult to correct. It's much easier to stay in alignment than to realign and fix the problems that resulted from the misalignment.

One way I do this regularly with God is to pray Psalm 139.23-24:

Search me, God, and know my heart;
   test me and know my anxious thoughts.
See if there is any offensive way in me,
   and lead me in the way everlasting.

And then I listen. I listen for God to speak to my heart, but I also realize that He may use others to speak to me, so I want to be sensitive to His voice, in whatever way it comes.

The Hebrew word for "anxious" in this text is the word śar-'ap-pāy meaning disquieting thoughts. (Studylight)

The Hebrew word for "offensive" in this text is the word 'ō·ṣeḇ which refers to deep pain. (Abarim)

So basically, I'm asking God to reveal anything in me that is not at peace. And then, is there anything in me that is causing deep pain for another? Followed up with a request to be aligned with Him. I wish I could say I do this every day or even every week, but I'm still working on it.

I want love, coming from a place of peace, to overflow from my life.

HE DELIGHTS IN OUR PROGRESS

As I type this, I'm making a new start with this. I'm encouraged, though, that I continue to make progress and I'm aligning with God more and more. I'm more aligned with Him today than I was ten years ago. I think He delights in our progress.

FREE

free

[frē]

VERB

1.a.   to cause to be free

  b.   to relieve or rid of what restrains, confines, restricts, or embarrasses

  c.   DISENTANGLE, CLEAR

18

IMPERFECT FREEDOM

"For you have been called to live in freedom...."
–Galatians 5.13a, NLT

*I*t's ironic. I'm in Chicago to focus on writing. I have total freedom, and I'm in a safe and secure hotel with staff taking care of my needs, and yet I don't feel free. It's January and cold outside, and I feel constrained even though I can come and go as I please and do whatever I want. It's not just the weather though. I've gone out and walked around during the day when the sun was out and the weather felt tolerable to be out. I stopped into Argo Tea (like a Starbucks for tea lovers) and hung out there for a bit. When I left my hotel room (with a view of a wall), I was surrounded by people, but I still felt isolated. Freedom felt trapped somewhere down deep inside me wanting to come out.

Where does a sense of freedom really come from? What does freedom really look like?

Freedom is actually void without security. Security is tolerable without freedom and it is enhanced with it.

But first, there has to be internal security and freedom for either to make a difference in our lives.

It's interesting—as I think about slavery in the south years ago, there were many who wanted to run away to be free—and with good reason. But once the law gave freedom to slaves, there were some who, having been treated well by their masters, opted to stay by free choice. For them, there was security in their free choice. They were finally able to experience external security and freedom.

But what about internal security and freedom? As I wrestled through my feelings while I was in Chicago and not feeling free, I sensed God speaking to me about the deeper issues connected to this. This is what I heard:

You are still flawed and imperfect. You still have struggles with discouragement and anxiety. I want you to understand how complete My love and acceptance are BEFORE you are as I created you to be. When you can experience my love and acceptance WITH your flaws, you will be in a place where you will be able to experience joy. Living in joy is one key to freedom. Understanding this will also allow you to love and accept others before they are perfected in who I created them to be.

We often want others to change so that we feel safe and secure. Galatians 5 seems to indicate that freedom grows when we care for each other and build each other up.

> It is absolutely clear that God has called you to a free life. Just make sure that you don't use this freedom as an excuse to do whatever you want to do and destroy your freedom. Rather, use your freedom to serve one another in love; that's how freedom grows. For everything we know about God's Word is summed up in a single sentence: Love others as you love yourself. That's an act of true freedom. If you bite and ravage each other, watch out—in no time at all you will be annihilating each other, and where will your precious freedom be then? –Galatians 5.13-15, MSG

As I'm looking at my heart, I'm seeing that it's broken in places—broken from what people have done to me, and broken from what other's have lacked in providing for me or others. Relationships are typically messy, and I tend to want to protect myself from the messiness that can be painful. I heard God speaking to my heart that I can release other people's limitations and let Him hold that. He will be their provision AND my provision. Then I'm free to love them without behavioral or heart expectations.

Lord, help me to let them be a mess—to even be imperfect and lacking.

PAIN MEMORIES

When I was young, there was someone I loved who expressed intense anger. When I saw it or experienced it, I felt very scared, unsafe emotionally, unprotected and uncared for. I was left with an emotional void. I felt alone with no one to help me through what I was feeling—the fear, the confusion, the loneliness, the uncertainty. It led me to a belief that where there is an expression of anger,

I'm not safe

I'm not cared for

I'm not emotionally protected

God reminded me that He was right there with me in those times—holding me and providing many sources of comfort so that I wouldn't be alone. Beth Moore says,

> The enemy wants you to believe you are alone; you're the only one; and to make you feel stupid. You are not alone in your struggle for freedom. You are surrounded by fellow strugglers. (Moore, Freedom)

And then I sensed God speaking this:

That person who expressed anger that scared you and left you feeling alone was not the enemy.

That person didn't make you feel alone or unprotected, unsafe or uncared for. That person felt all those same things, and you saw how they responded to their own painful feelings.

Your enemy (and that person's enemy) is the one who convinced each of you of the lies that perpetuated each of your pain. Satan convinced both of you and used you against each other. He set you up to make you enemies when, in fact, he is the source of your pain—your true enemy.

For our struggle is not against flesh and blood, but against the rulers, against the authorities, against the powers of this dark world and against the spiritual forces of evil in the heavenly realms. (Ephesians 6.12)

SHAME MEMORIES

What is the opposite of freedom? Slavery, right? Galatians 5.1, ESV says, "For freedom Christ has set us free; stand firm therefore, and do not submit again to a yoke of slavery." I want to clear out everything that leads me back to a yoke of slavery—whether it's my fleshly desires, selfishness, pride, etc. so that God's Spirit can be released in me so that I can live in freedom.

If, as God's Word says, the truth will set us free (John 8.32), then it's lies that hold us in slavery or bondage. One way to identify lies is to take a look at where you feel shame, because shame and lies are often closely connected.

As I was scanning my shame memories, I landed on an area of shame from nearly 20 years ago. As I look at it now, I don't know why I ever felt shame, but back then, several years after my lifeguarding years (where my feet were always exposed and I was fine with it), I found myself ashamed of my feet. I wouldn't go barefoot or be in a situation that revealed my feet.

One day I was planning to visit my friend Lora. When I got to her house, we sat down on the couch, and then she pulled out a basket filled with many different colors of nail polish and suggested we paint our toe nails. I quickly declined and would not be moved by her prompting. Nonetheless, I believe she knew that my inhibition was shame-based, so she persisted to the point of grabbing my feet and pulling my socks off. Then, looking at my feet, she gently spoke, "Why are you ashamed of your feet? You have beautiful feet." I immediately experienced freedom.

> SHAME WAS A LIE THAT TOLD ME I WOULD BE UNACCEPTED

Shame was a lie that told me I would be unaccepted, mocked and unloved. But in just one quick moment, the shame and the lies were dispelled, and truth was restored. The truth was that although beauty is in the eye of the beholder, someone AND Someone saw my feet as beautiful. And with that truth giving me confidence, I was able to begin living in freedom. I could go barefoot if I wanted to; I could get a pedicure; I could have complete peace whether my feet were exposed or not.

Not all freedom is so immediate. Some freedom takes time. At LifeCare we talk about God healing in Power or in Process. Beth Moore refers to it as healing in Supremacy or Sufficiency. Regardless of the term, in the former, it is an immediate experience of His power. In the latter, we learn to find our sufficiency in Him through the process of healing a particular area of our lives. In finding our sufficiency in Him, we learn to know and love and trust Him step by step, more and more deeply. He has purpose in both types of healing.

BUTTERFLIES

I look at butterflies differently now. Today, as I watched a butterfly bouncing around, seemingly aimlessly, I realized that I see them differently than I used to. This is not merely a butterfly—it is a caterpillar with wings. It is a caterpillar that is no longer confined to the ground or a branch of a tree but is now free to roam the sky as well. If I suddenly experienced that kind of freedom, I would probably flutter around in tremendous excitement as well.

The good news is that's exactly what God intends. In Isaiah, the prophet expresses the ability of a child of

God: "I will rise up with wings like eagles...." We have the ability to soar even higher than I imagine a butterfly can. But with the same sort of exciting freedom that the butterfly has in roaming from flower to flower, taking in the captivating beauty and delightful fragrance of each one.

In order to experience that kind of freedom though, we must cooperate with His plan and strategy as He intentionally strips us of the layers that hold us down.

"But those who wait for the LORD's help find renewed strength; they rise up as if they had eagles' wings...."
–Isaiah 40.31a, NET

19

THE PATH THAT LEADS TO LIFE

"Therefore, there is now no
condemnation for those who are in Christ
Jesus." –Romans 8.1

As a child of God, we may hunger for certain things (be it substances, circumstances, possessions, relationships, ...) and we may condemn ourselves because of a hunger that is in conflict with our desire to make God our first love. God, however, does not condemn us. Our own hearts may condemn us, but He is bigger than our hearts. 1 John 3.19-20 says,

> This is how we know that we belong to the truth and how we set our hearts at rest in his presence: If our hearts condemn us, we know that God is greater than our hearts, and he knows everything.

His heart is filled with love and compassion for us. He actually gave us His Spirit that makes us aware of choices we make and desires we have that are not aligned with Him—not so we'll feel bad, but so we'll know the right way to go—the path that leads to Life. Then as we have the awareness of the right way to go, we can choose to go that way.

PURPOSE

Several years ago, my parents bought some property for hunting. As a bonus, it came with a house that they began to fix up. When I'm in town, I like to stay at that house for the solitude and connection with God that I have there. One day when I was there, I was sitting alone out on the deck overlooking the river, 68 degrees, the sun rising, birds chirping, gentle sounds of the water quietly flowing down the river, a black squirrel climbing in the tree next to me...and my soul speaking, "This is life." But that voice was interrupted by what I believe was God's voice speaking:

This is a break from life. This life is hard. It has trouble, but I walk you through each trouble. Today I'm providing a break for you with the beauty of My creation. One day, when your time in this life is done, you will experience the complete fullness of what I intended for you...even beyond what you're experiencing today. But today I will provide refreshment for you—tastes of My glory—tastes of eternity— as you go through this life.

If I keep looking for this experience (and other experiences of comfort and refreshment) to BE my life, I will be frustrated and miss all that God has for me to be and do in this life, as He walks beside me, leading me.

TRUSTING GOD'S HEART...
WHEN IT'S HARD TO TRUST HIS HAND

Skimming the first few chapters of the book of Ezekiel (NLT), I noticed the various things that Ezekiel said he felt or experienced. God had called Ezekiel to the task of giving messages to His people, the nation of Israel, who had been hard-hearted and rebellious since the very beginning. The messages would be difficult and not pleasant at all. God also informed Ezekiel that the people would not receive the messages, but not to fear them, not to be afraid of their threats, and not to be dismayed by their dark scowls. (Ezekiel 2.6)

God first gave Ezekiel a scroll of His first message and told him to "eat" it. Glancing at it, Ezekiel saw that the scroll was "covered with funeral songs, other words of sorrow, and pronouncements of doom." (2.10b) But upon eating it, Ezekiel said that "it tasted as **sweet** as honey...." (3.3b) I'll come back to that.

After taking time to let the words sink deep into his own heart as God instructed, God then lifted him up and took him away. Ezekiel said he "went in **bitterness** and **turmoil**" (3.14), and when he came to the exiles, he "was **overwhelmed** and sat among them for seven days." (3.15b)

Sweet, bitterness, turmoil and overwhelmed. The task he had was extremely difficult resulting in his feelings of bitterness, turmoil and being overwhelmed. But what's interesting is that when he was in God's presence with God's words, even God's difficult, painful words of correction and doom were experienced by Ezekiel as sweet.

I believe God chose Ezekiel because his heart was soft. Because his heart was soft, Ezekiel knew that God's heart was sweet and he was able to experience the sweetness of God's heart. God's heart in this was to pour out discipline, correction and doom for the sole purpose of redemption. He wanted their wayward, rebellious hearts to turn back to Him; He longed for the heart of His bride. He let Ezekiel know that although most of the people

HE KNEW THAT THERE WAS SWEETNESS IN GOD'S PRESENCE

would continue in their rebellion, "some of them will listen." (3.27, GNT) Ezekiel knew that even though his task brought feelings of bitterness, turmoil and being overwhelmed, he also knew that there was sweetness in God's presence, in His words and in His heart. Ezekiel could move forward in the difficulty of God's plan knowing he could confidently rest on God's heart.

Sometimes God calls us to do things that are unpleasant and difficult. Being God's voice isn't always a welcomed thing, and (because some people are hard-hearted) it can even bring turmoil our way. But we can have confidence in knowing God's heart and the sweetness of His presence.

TRUTH OR REFLECTION

When we face difficulties like Ezekiel did, and especially when other people don't respond favorably to us, we can often tend to base our reality on how others respond to us. But the truth is, how they respond or react to us is a complete reflection of what they're dealing with. Truth is what God speaks about me and is doing in and around me. Like Ezekiel, others' reactions may not always feel good, but I can have confidence in God's heart for me.

20

DESERT OF FULFILLMENT

"You set your people free, and you led
them through the desert."
–Psalm 68.7, CEV

ometimes I feel like I'm in a lonely desert:
Even the Psalmist in Psalm 102:6 (CEV)
lamented, "I am like a lonely owl in the desert".
But as I looked into it more deeply, God called people
(Moses, Israel, even Jesus) into the desert, and He met
them there. Even Hagar, who ran away, He met in the
desert. God freed the Israelites by taking them out of
Egypt and into the desert.

Take a look at the following verses:

Deuteronomy 1:31 (CEV), "And you know that the
Lord has taken care of us the whole time we've been in
the desert, just as you might carry one of your children."

Nehemiah 9:19 (CEV), "Because of your great mercy,
you never abandoned them in the desert."

Psalm 68:7 (CEV), "You set your people free, and you led them through the desert."

CRAVINGS

In our times of need—in our desert experiences, our cravings, apart from God, are most likely to be revealed. Psalm 106:14 says, "In the desert they gave in to their craving; in the wilderness they put God to the test." In a desert place, God can reveal those illegitimate cravings and bring healing. He can bring truth about what drives our cravings and fears, and sufficiency in who He is and can be in our lives. He can bring us so much love in our desert places:

Psalm 107:35 (CEV), "But the Lord can also turn deserts into lakes and scorched land into flowing streams."

Psalm 136:16 (CEV), "The Lord led his people through the desert. God's love never fails."

Beth Moore says, "Anytime you can't get enough of anything, you are missing something." (Moore, Freedom) She talked about the one woman who took a bucket for water and went to a nearby well. Jesus was there and had a conversation with her. He exposed her craving when he talked of how she had been married five times, and the man she's now living with isn't her husband. She came to the well not just with an empty water bucket, but also with an empty soul. Beth Moore goes on to say that "You have to be fully engaged with Jesus for your life to be full."

Cravings feel like a desert. They reveal that I'm lacking something—often a core need, but the craving is usually for something different, something that would tend to provide a similar impact but in a less than ideal, illegitimate way.

The woman at the well had a deep need—a soul craving that she was trying to fill with a husband. In a physical way, I may crave chocolate when my core need is for magnesium. Or if my legitimate emotional need is for acceptance, I may crave the party scene because I've learned that I'm accepted there, or maybe I would crave one-on-one time with someone in particular who has made me feel accepted.

Years ago, I remember often having a craving to watch movies with a friend. The core need was for legitimate healthy touch. My friend enjoyed giving healthy touch (back rubs in particular) and especially during movie watching. Rather than acknowledge my core need, I would suggest watching a movie—out of fear, mostly. I was afraid to acknowledge my true need, so I wasn't being honest or authentic about my true needs. I also wasn't trusting God and going to Him first with my need and trusting however He wanted to meet it, which is critical.

When I hold my authentic desert cravings up to God, I'm able to find the kind of refreshment that He wants to provide for me.

THE WILDERNESS

The wilderness has a lot of similarities to the desert, but the wilderness, to me, feels cold and like I'm even more unable to find my way. At one point several years ago, I thought I was living in an emotional wilderness— longing for more—more of something, and trying to fill the wilderness with things and people I thought God was providing.

I visited the Grand Canyon for the first time and was able to take a few minutes to just sit at the edge of the Grand Canyon and listen to God, whatever He wanted to speak to me. It was a cold day in November, and sitting outside for very long wasn't all that inviting. But as I listened, I heard Him speak about the wilderness and how I'd taken so many pictures the last few days of the desert, the wilderness, and lonely and seemingly desolate places. I took pictures because I saw so much beauty in those places—especially where the sunlight (Son-light) scattered a vast array of beams and projected shadows of beauty in various ways depending on the time of day and configuration of clouds. The beauty was endless. As I sat at the edge of possibly the most beautiful wilderness on earth, He reminded me of the wealth of beauty that He can bring from the lonely, desolate wilderness.

I sensed Him drawing me more deeply into His presence, calling me into the wilderness to be with Him there—much like Jesus got away in the wilderness and went to "lonely" places to be with His Father. I've avoided those places because lonely places do not sound nice or appealing—they sound painful to the soul. But therein lies the paradox of the spiritual life—what we think will bring life, instead brings death; and what we think brings death, will actually bring life.

Later, God took it a step further with me. I had been thinking that I was already in the wilderness and trying to fill it. Instead, I had been stuffed so full of activity and responsibilities and more and more ideas and aspirations that it stuffed me and weighed me down. Rather than finding more to satisfy me, I needed a spiritual detox that could only be found in the beauty of the wilderness and the peacefulness of dry, lonely, desolate places where God's voice can be heard and His presence felt, and where I leave room for Him to come and abide with me and envelop me.

"'I will even make a way in the wilderness, and rivers in the desert.'" –Isaiah 43.19b, ASV

MORE THAN I HAVE

I emailed a friend and shared with her about an area of temptation where I was struggling, and action steps I was taking to deal righteously with it. In her response, she said, "You are obviously in need of something. Search your heart."

EMPTINESS TENDS TO CAUSE ME TO LONG FOR SOMETHING MORE THAN I HAVE

In my searching, I found areas of emptiness. Emptiness tends to cause me to long for something more than I have. Jesus said, "I came that they may have life, and may have it abundantly." (John 10.10b, ASV). In that abundance, I will have freedom. In the emptiness, I experience oppression, heaviness, fear—in short, bondage.

Many of the things that Jesus cautioned against were things that people use to try to fill emptiness:

Jealousy says that I am not enough unless I have what you have that I'm lacking, so there's an emptiness that I have to fill by getting what you have.

Greed says I am not enough with just what I have, so there's an emptiness that I have to fill by getting more and more.

Immorality says I am not enough by doing what's good and right, so there's an emptiness that I have to fill by doing what's wrong.

Adultery says that the one I have isn't enough for me, and that God's boundaries are too constricting and don't provide me with enough, so there's an emptiness that I have to fill by seeking another.

Theft says I don't feel powerful enough, and I'm entitled to something more than I earn or buy, so there's an emptiness that I have to fill by taking what is not mine.

Pride says I am not enough to live confidently apart from building myself up, so there's an emptiness that I have to fill by elevating myself.

Malice says I am not enough to live powerfully apart from tearing you down, so there's an emptiness that I have to fill by doing harm.

Deceit says I am not enough to live authentically, so there's an emptiness that I have to fill through deception.

So how do I get the abundance that Jesus talked about so that I'm not pursuing the wrong things out of my emptiness?

The woman at the well went to the well with an empty bucket and an empty life. She was empty and trying to fill that emptiness with men. But it hadn't worked.

When she met Jesus at the well, and He began to tell her the truth about herself, it shocked her in a refreshing way. Jesus says the truth will set us free (John 8.32). He was giving her a taste of the truth that she needed in order to be set free, and with just a taste of truth, she was experiencing hope, life—a taste of freedom.

We don't know exactly what happened in her life after that encounter with Jesus. I suspect, though, that she experienced hope and was motivated to make changes in her life and seek more truth in order to walk consistently in freedom. He told her that those who worship God "'must worship in the Spirit and in truth.'" (John 4.24) Truth would bring her freedom; her emptiness was the result of believing lies. One, in particular, was the lie of adultery:

Adultery says that the one I have isn't enough for me, and that God's boundaries are too constricting and don't provide me with enough, so there's an emptiness that I have to fill by seeking another.

By seeking God to speak into her belief about her emptiness, she would hear His truth for her and she would be transformed by the renewing of her mind. Freedom would result.

CANAAN IN THE DESERT

Sitting by the fountain at the garden of Jesus' suffering and resurrection at *Canaan in the Desert* in Phoenix, my heart is refreshed. This is a cool place. The gardens tell the story of Jesus' life, death and resurrection. There are compartments you can open to get a word. My word was "Sacrifice".

As I'm resting and meditating, I'm hearing, "Be still and know that I am God." I've had a hard time connecting with God lately, but I've also had a hard time just sitting and listening in a quiet undistracted place where I can focus on Him.

Even when I've gotten alone lately, I haven't been still. I haven't released myself—my troubles, my anxiety, the things I feel like I have to fix. They've kept me distracted and prevented me from being still.

This place helps. In front of me, there are names for God etched into the concrete fountain. Names such as, "Father of Goodness" and "Father of Faithfulness".

I remember words from a song, "You are good, You are good when there's nothing good in me...." (Forever Reign)

I can't fix the things and people surrounding my life. Like my "French fry story" that I shared in my previous book, *Loved As I Should Have Been*, all I can do is hold them up to God and ask Him what He wants to do with them. And then I can watch what He does, trusting and knowing that He will do something amazing.

As I walked over to a prayer bench, a sign read,

"I will bless the Lord at all times." –Psalm 34:1 God's will is goodness and lovingkindness, and good are the paths He leads us on.

Whatever I do, I KNOW that treating others with goodness and lovingkindness is God's plan for me, and the path He has me on is good.

Sitting in another place, the marker read,

My Father, I do not understand you, but I trust you!

Another song came to mind, "I worship You, almighty God, there is none like You. I worship You, oh Prince of peace; that is what I want to do. I give You praise for You are my righteousness." (I Worship You)

Jesus also met me in this desert place in Phoenix, and He refreshed me!

21

DISTRACTED: "SQUIRREL!"

"For you are God, my only safe haven."
–Psalm 43.2a, NLT

I know that sometimes with our friends, we can enjoy them, appreciate them and love them, and yet still lose connection with them. In those times, when our lives don't overlap naturally, we have to be more intentional about connecting with each other.

For many years, I've connected with God daily and have even learned to stay aware of His presence and talk to Him continually as I've gone through my day. But I noticed that at one point I was distracted a lot. I would go to a park to spend some quality, focused time with Him, and I would get distracted by the squirrels and other wildlife, the other people, trees, Facebook, just about everything besides God. I noticed my distraction and difficulty focusing and started to get more determined to try harder. But it kept happening.

I knew there were some things I needed to deal with in my life—things that were not as they should be, and I knew I needed God's help. So I tried to talk through this with God by looking at what I was feeling in order to discover what I was believing about certain things in my life that weren't peaceful. But I still couldn't focus, so I asked a friend to help me. I met with her and shared with her what was troubling to me. I even shared about things I was reading in my Bible that were making me angry with God. Things like Psalm 43.2 (NLT):

For you are God, my only safe haven. Why have you tossed me aside? Why must I wander around in darkness, oppressed by my enemies?

My response to God was:

You are not safe! I DO feel like You've tossed me aside, and You're leaving me in darkness and allowing me to be oppressed by lies that are my enemies—lies that are consuming me! You are not safe, and I'm angry with You!

I was filled with intense emotion. My friend prayed for me before we began to take a closer look at my painful feelings and uncover lies I might be believing. She finished praying and asked what I was currently feeling. I said, "Peace. I actually feel like I'm on vacation, maybe in Florida, and everything's good. But," I continued, "I also know that that's what my mind has been doing. I start to get in touch with the negative feelings and then find an escape, but I really do want truth and healing."

So she asked me what I had been feeling as I was driving there. Immediately, I was in touch with my emotions again and we went on to discover things I was believing that stirred up negative emotion. Something that stood out to me was this: When I'm not at peace with God, I will run away from Him rather than TO Him for safety, security and truth. That's the main reason I couldn't focus on Him and I was so distracted by everything in my environment—even good things. But I was distracted FROM what was best.

Over the next several days, my anger toward God actually got worse, and I became edgy with others as well.

SILENCING GOD

I became a Christian when I was eight years old; I can't remember what it was like to be without God. I've always valued His presence, but I guess I never really grasped the magnitude of His presence in my life—I suppose I didn't have anything to actually compare it to—until now.

In writing this book, I have come face to face with some inner turmoil having to do with a little more aftermath from my childhood sexual abuse. At one point, I became very angry with God. As I stood face to face with my darkness, I was overwhelmed and bitter. I lashed out at God, but He met me in my anger and spoke firmly yet tenderly to me. I wrestled with Him in it, but I also began to turn from Him. I didn't notice it clearly at the time, but my anger and distrust grew quickly, and I sought my own relief in subtle ways.

As I shook my fist at Him for leaving me in darkness, it took a toll on my body. Headaches were almost constant, tension and pain through my neck and shoulders left me with restless nights and in search of some sort of healthy means of relief. I became edgy and miserable and lost. I literally felt like I was on a road toward death.

I had never really turned from God before, but for four days I did. During those four days I was in a spiritual grave.

I accused Him.

I turned from Him.

I left Him.

And I was miserable!

RESURRECTION

Like Lazarus, though, after four days, God brought about my resurrection.

I don't go to a lot of concerts, but my friend had been planning on going to an Outcry concert locally with her husband. At the last minute, he was unable to go, so she invited me. Even though my heart was hard and bitter, I thought the time with my friend would be nice. So I went.

I'm not exaggerating at all when I say that every single song for the first two-thirds of the concert gripped my heart, tenderly and powerfully breaking up the hardness that had begun to cover and toughen it.

> The first song was THERE IS A CLOUD.
>> Hear the Word, roaring as thunder
>> With a new future to tell
>> For the dry season is over
>> There is a cloud beginning to swell
>> ...Every seed buried in sorrow
>> You will call forth in its time
>> You are Lord, Lord of the harvest
>> Calling our hope, now to arise
>> We receive Your rain
>> We receive Your rain

Then, HERE AS IN HEAVEN, which starts out, "The atmosphere is changing now...." Followed by, O COME TO THE ALTAR:

> Are you hurting and broken within?
> Overwhelmed by the weight of your sin?
> Jesus is calling
> Have you come to the end of yourself?
> Do you thirst for a drink from the well?
> Jesus is calling

Then, RESURRECTING.
    The fear that held us now gives way
    To Him who is our peace
    His final breath upon the cross
    Is now alive in me
    Your name, Your name
    Is victory
    All praise, will rise
    To Christ, our king
    By Your spirit I will rise
    From the ashes of defeat
    The resurrected King is resurrecting me
    In Your name I come alive
    To declare Your victory
    The resurrected King is resurrecting me

And COME ALIVE (DRY BONES).
    Through the eyes of men it seems
    There's so much we have lost
    As we look down the road
    Where all the prodigals have walked
    One by one
    The enemy has whispered lies
    And led them off as slaves

    But we know that You are God
    Yours is the victory
    We know there is more to come
    That we may not yet see

So with the faith You've given us
We'll step into the valley unafraid
...
God of endless mercy
God of unrelenting love
Rescue every daughter
Bring us back the wayward son
And by Your spirit breathe upon them
Show the world that You alone can save
You alone can save

As we call out to dry bones
Come alive, come alive
We call out to dead hearts
Come alive, come alive
Up out of the ashes
Let us see an army rise
We call out to dry bones come alive

And those were just some of the songs that He used to draw my dead heart back to life. Once I was able to hear His tender words of truth again and turn back to Him and receive His love, it was then that I realized I was a prodigal. I had run away from Him, and for the first time that I could remember, I understood what it was like to be without Christ; to be without the safety and security that I had always leaned on. And I was tightly wrapped in painful, debilitating bondage (grave clothes) as a result. Like Peter, I denied Christ. Like the Prodigal, I was angry and bitter and ran away from my Father, refusing His love. It was possibly the most miserable time in my life. I needed a safe place, and I no longer had one. I needed security, and it was gone. I pushed both out of my life.

But also like the Prodigal, I came back to His unconditional acceptance and love. And like Peter, I felt so much shame that I could deny His place in my life. But His response to me was so beautiful, so alluring, drawing me tenderly back into His arms of love, bringing light to my darkness, restoring hope and joy to me once again.

I think of Sarah's maidservant, Hagar, who ran away and then ran into God who had gone after her to draw her back. She gave God a new name that was precious to her and spoke to her need. She called Him "The God Who Sees Me"; she needed to be seen.

After reconnecting with God myself, I could finally allow myself to be held and tenderly embraced by God again—but in a new way that was more authentic and tender than ever before. I needed that. And I, too, gave God a new name—one that was precious to me and spoke to my need: "Jehovah Habaq", "The God Who Holds Me". In His tender, loving, forgiving embrace, He's restored my joy and hope, and He's given me my song again. He's the God of my song.

I'm so in love with Him. I now see how much I've been forgiven, and I'm imagining washing His feet with my tears because He has rescued me, restored to me safety and security, and taken me out of the miserable state I was in. I never want to go back to that.

I shared all this with my husband, and when I was done sharing, he prayed for me. As he began to pray, it began to rain outside. I had the window open and I could hear it clearly. Then as soon as he was done praying, the rain stopped. To me, it was a beautiful symbol of God showing up with nourishment, refreshment and promise.

"The dry season is over; there is a cloud beginning to swell."

22

FLAWED

"'In this world, you will have trouble. But take heart! I have overcome the world.'"
–John 16.33b

What if you're not what you think you are? Sometimes, out of fear, we may present ourselves in a way that appears quite adequate, maybe even perfect. But what if that's not who we really are? What if I'm really not as good as I portray or want to believe? What if I'm more flawed than would be acceptable? What if what is in me is actually something bad, or something corrupt, or something less than acceptable?

I remember years ago someone commented to me, "You're too perfect." It made me take a step back and evaluate. I certainly knew I wasn't perfect, but at the same time I was deeply afraid of allowing my shortcomings to be seen. So I avoided doing things that others would see until I had perfected them enough.

Needless to say, it left me very restrained and limited in the things I did, and very much lacking freedom. I have found over the years that there's so much freedom in being able to let myself be wrong, or flawed and not have to try to show how right I am or try to look better than I am.

There's freedom in being able to laugh at myself when I try to sing and start on the wrong note (and it happened to be while leading worship!).

There's freedom in not knowing how to do something and yet trying to do it but falling down and letting someone reach down and help me up.

There's freedom in thinking you heard one thing and finding out it was another, but finding humor in it. My hearing isn't what it used to be, and it's humbling to acknowledge that I have that flaw. But humbling doesn't have to be shameful; we can actually find humor in our humility.

WE CAN ACTUALLY FIND HUMOR IN OUR HUMILITY

One day, and I actually do this often now, rather than get frustrated because I couldn't quite make out what my friend said, I tried to repeat back what I thought I heard. My friend was with me and we had picked up some things at some stores, and then I pulled into her driveway to drop her off at home. She opened her door and got out of the passenger's side. As she was turned away from me, she said something that I could almost—but not quite—make out. I repeated back to her what I thought I heard her say: "Am I drunk?" She started laughing and repeated, "No, can you open your trunk?" A few years later, we are still laughing about that interaction.

Just tonight, I had a fire going in the fireplace and my husband walked into the room holding a box. He said something, and I heard most of what he said. I repeated what I thought I heard: "Do I want a box of toilet paper from work?" He clarified, "a box of cardboard and paper." We laughed.

I'm flawed, I know it, and I no longer want to try to hide it. I want to humbly acknowledge where I'm flawed, rolling with it, and confident that as I peacefully offer my flaws to God, He will use them in delightful ways that I never expected.

Even with my gifts, my humanity ensures that I'm flawed there too. But it's still okay.

THEY CAN RELATE MORE TO FLAWS THAN PERFECTION

And I've found that people are actually encouraged more when I'm not portraying or insisting on my perfection—they can relate more to flaws than perfection, and relating helps connection in relationship.

So what about your flaws? Sometimes we have flaws in our strengths, gifts and abilities. There are times when what we believe we hear from God may not be purely from Him but intertwined with our fears or longings. I want to be at peace with whatever flaws I have, but sometimes it's unsettling. If I'm lacking peace though, I know I can ask God to help me to see why.

What do you believe flaws communicate about you? Do you believe that if you have flaws, you'll be rejected or humiliated?

Humble may be the root word of humiliated; however, they are so different. Sometimes it's shame that's associated with humiliation and other times it's actually arrogance that is more closely associated with humiliation, and yet it oftentimes feels like the opposite is true. Being humble, though, is honorable and impressive.

A SINFUL WOMAN

Some of us know we're broken, and we've had sinful patterns that we've used to cope with our brokenness. When we know these things about ourselves and believe others see them and condemn us, we may have a tendency to hide. It's safer, after all.

There's the story in Luke 7.36-50 where Jesus was invited to a Pharisee's house for a meal. Jesus went. A woman went as well when she heard Jesus was there. She went in and knelt behind Him, washing His feet with her tears.

Why did she want to be where He was?

Why did she do what she did?

Why was she crying?

Maybe she knew His heart. Maybe she knew that He would love and accept her as she was. Maybe she saw how He could fill and redeem her life despite her history. Maybe she was drawn to the sweetness of His character that overshadowed everything she had ever been or done. Maybe that drew her out of hiding.

The Pharisee, on the other hand, condemned her. He only saw that she wasn't good enough to be in His presence. What he didn't see, though, was that he also was not good enough to be in Jesus' presence, yet Jesus valued them both equally, but highlighted the truth that she actually loved Him more.

Had she listened to the messages of those who condemned her, she never would have come out of hiding. But instead, she focused on the voice of the One who saw beyond her faults and knew her heart. She focused on the sweetness of Jesus' character, and that drew her out of hiding—to live authentically and beautifully.

In order to stay out of hiding and to move into the person that God intended for me to be, I have to own and embrace who God says I am. I will live out who I believe I am. So if I'm listening to the Pharisee, and choosing to believe the Pharisee's words about me— that I'm unacceptable and unworthy, I will live that out in my life. God knows exactly who I am, and yet He has made me new, and He embraces me with sweetness and acceptance, drawing me into His presence to be even more beautiful. I will choose to believe who God says I am.

FEAR

Just before I woke up one morning, I had this very brief "dream." In the dream I got an email from a friend, and all I saw before waking up was: "I'm disappointed that you...." And then I woke up feeling very distraught.

I knew it wasn't guilt but had to do with a fear that I've had as long as I can remember. At times, when I hear an email come in or my phone rings or I get a text, there's an underlying fear of someone expressing disappointment or disapproval in some way regarding something I did. I think this is what has inhibited me in making confident decisions at various times. Apparently, the fear even lingers in my sleep.

I began to process my thoughts with God and recognized that I had been kind of afraid of making the "wrong" decision at times. Thinking through it, I asked myself, "If I made the wrong decision, what would that mean?" My answer: "It would mean I'd be leading people in the wrong direction."

When I was young, I didn't want to be a teacher in any respect because I was so afraid of leading someone in the wrong direction and messing up their life. I respected teachers and valued them but believed I would fail anyone I taught or led if I made any mistake.

I had forgotten about this but I remember it being such a huge thing (a vow maybe) in my life when I was young.

Interestingly, as I look back, I can see so many times when I was guided into or drawn into teaching or leadership in some way. Renee was my swim coach, and she offered to pay me to help her teach some swimming classes when I was 16. Because of the powerful influence of one of my English teachers my senior year of high school, I decided to move toward getting a teaching degree in communications, because I wanted to impact people like she impacted me. Just out of college, though, a friend helped me secure a job as a work floor supervisor in a sheltered workshop which quickly led to being offered a position as a job coach for mentally ill and developmentally disabled adults—a highly instructional position.

WHILE GOD LED ME, SATAN RESTRAINED ME

Looking back, I see God's guidance in putting me in these and many other instructional, influential or leadership positions, but while God led me, Satan restrained me with lies. Still, God has remained sovereign and has worked through it all.

Going back to my fear of someone's disappointment or disapproval though, my deeper fear was of leading someone in the wrong direction and messing up their life.

What's the truth?

This is what I sensed from God:

Regardless of your choices or direction for others, I AM sovereign. Joseph's brothers could have completely messed up Joseph's life, but I saw how to accomplish my intentions through their imperfect—and even evil—choices. In your wounded leadership, you will make great choices AND poor choices, but I will accomplish My purposes through all of them. I just want you to keep moving—and I'll take care of the results. I've got this!

MORE FEAR

I received a real email from this same friend that I dreamt emailed me. She was responding to a prayer list I had put together for several people, and had replied saying, "My stuff is out of date." There was more that followed, but I couldn't seem to hear anything beyond that first line.

What I heard was, "I'm disappointed in you." And then I heard, "I'm angry with you", which to me means I won't be cared for.

I processed my thoughts and explored some memories that connected with these feelings— memories where I had experienced anger from a couple different people where it felt like they hated me and that nothing I could do would please them.

God, in His grace, showed me that it was their pain speaking, not their true heart.

I recognized that there was a lie that I believed that someone's disappointment in something I did = I AM a disappointment, I am hated, I will be unloved, I will lose privileges or not receive desires, I will not be cared for.

Recognizing the truth freed me, so that now, as I re-read my friend's email that says, "My stuff is out of date", what I hear is that her stuff is out of date and it would be good to get it updated. That's it.

REGRETS

I felt heaviness as I thought about some things I wish I had the opportunity to do over. Regrets seem to have the power to hold me in bondage.

I wish I would have celebrated a specific accomplishment of one of my sons. I wish I would have stayed in my friend's wedding as her bridesmaid rather than bowing out because I was overwhelmed with other areas of my life. I wish I would have been a better example to my kids in various ways. I wish I could do that interview over and not be so nervous this time. I wish I would have replied to that accusation a different way. I wish I would have been more confident in my skills and abilities when I tried to answer that question. I wish I wouldn't have been afraid to try that, to speak up, to move out of my comfort zone.

We can really beat ourselves up for the mistakes we've made or the things we would do differently if we could do them over. Pondering some of these things, I was in tears feeling like I ruined my son's life because, looking back, I didn't celebrate something I thought should have been celebrated. I was in tears because, looking back, I felt like I completely betrayed a friend by bowing out of her wedding.

God spoke freedom over me, however, when He reminded me that He is bigger than my shortcomings and He is sovereign over my failures. I can't mess up more than He can clean up. He can redeem ANY mess I give Him. And then I remembered Romans 8.28:

> So we are convinced that every detail of our lives is continually woven together to fit into God's perfect plan of bringing good into our lives, for we are his lovers who have been called to fulfill his designed purpose. (TPT)

I CAN'T MESS UP
MORE THAN HE CAN CLEAN UP

23

MORE THAN I'VE LOST

"Instead of your shame
you will receive a double portion,
and instead of disgrace
you will rejoice in your inheritance.
And so you will inherit a double portion in
your land,
and everlasting joy will be yours."
–Isaiah 61.7

As I lean into God, sharing my pain with Him, He will carry it for me, freeing me to live without retaliation, vengeance, frustration or edginess because I can have confidence that God is caring for my wounds and will restore much more than I've lost. (Isaiah 61.1-7) Knowing that, I can more easily, confidently and freely pour out unconditional love on those who hurt me (whether intentional or not). In theory, at least. It's hard to live out—I certainly know that.

LIKE YOU'VE NEVER BEEN HURT

I've been recognizing lately how God has been helping me to pray. I was just talking to Him about how, as I get older, it seems like it's harder and harder to really love people as He loves. So I was asking Him about that and wanted Him to empower me to love as He loves. I was recognizing that, through the years, we carry more and more people-wounds—and it impacts us. Then very specifically I heard, "Love like you've never been hurt." I suppose if I approach people from that perspective, it changes everything. And even though I may get hurt, I have a God who takes care of me.

GOOD GRIEF!

Sometimes there are things that we wish would be different from what they are. Maybe it's as big as grieving the loss of a loved one, or maybe it's as small as lamenting that events we go to are too big or too small for our preference. Or maybe that every time we get a vacation or a break, when we come back we end up with more work.

Sometimes we need to consciously choose gratitude for the good, and hold our hands open regarding what we see as bad.

Our ongoing grief and lamenting and frustration with the way things are that we can't control steal our peace and joy. God has already gone before us and knows everything that we will walk into—everything we will face, and He says about it, "'For I know the plans I have for you,...plans to prosper you and not to harm you, plans to give you hope and a future.'" (Jeremiah 29.11) Not everything we face is good in itself, but when we entrust it to God's hands, He makes even the bad things work in our favor.

When a loved one dies, it is certainly important for us to grieve that loss. Letting go of what we had and what we had hoped for in the future can be extremely difficult. I was thinking about the way people say, "Rest In Peace" when someone dies.

GO

IN

PEACE

Although very hard, it seems that one way to allow someone to rest in peace is when we, ourselves, "Go In Peace" from what we shared with that person. If we, instead, shake our fist at the One who could have provided a different outcome—the One who still has a good plan—we let the enemy steal our joy and the beautiful history that we had that can propel us into a strong future.

The same is true for anything that feels like a loss or feels like it's not enough. Feeling a time of sadness for what we lack is important. Joyfully remembering how God has enriched our lives is critical to our peace. Easy to say, right?

When my brother fought cancer at 40 years old, I grieved and lamented with a broken heart as he battled that monster. Although I couldn't be with him often, when I could be, I held his hand, I smiled with him, I cried with him. When he could no longer speak, I held his hand and looked into his bright blue eyes—the eyes that held so many rich memories. After his death, memories rolled through my mind and still continue to many years later. Memories of how he enhanced my life in so many ways. Memories of gratitude; memories of pain; memories of being a family—but all memories of significance. I wish we would have had many more years together, but I can move forward in my own life a little stronger and a little better because he was a part of my life. That helps me to move forward in peace.

TRANSFORM

Many things can wound our soul. Certainly death, but also betrayal, abuse of any kind, deception, neglect, ... Usually we long for peace. Moving forward in peace happens by transforming our mind. Transforming our mind allows us to see the goodness of God. In order to transform our mind, though, we have to understand what we believe that doesn't line up with God's mind.

We can't just muster up joy—it's a fruit of the spirit. But it is worship to the Lord to cry out to Him. Our worship of crying out to Him can actually result in joy: Psalm 126.5 (AMP) says, "They who sow in tears shall reap with joyful singing."

There can be gifts in all of our emotions if we yield to God's intention.

If we feel our...		it can lead to...
Shame	→	humility and compassion
Loneliness	→	reaching out
Sadness	→	healing
Fear	→	wisdom and courage
Anger	→	strength and justice

What has wounded your soul? You may want to ask God to lead you to the gift that He has for you as you lay out your wounds for Him to hold.

SEARCH ME

Satan wants us separated from God—to keep us from God's gift and blessing of abundant life. Satan can accomplish that separation using our self-confidence so we don't think we need God, or despair so we can't trust God.

Our spirit is broken if we're believing things that are contrary to the Truth/character of God. We may want to be healed, but we may not want to be searched (Psalm 139). It hurts to be searched sometimes. Some searching is intense. Many times, though, trying to cope with our wounds and brokenness is actually more painful than being searched.

I dealt with the pain of sciatica occasionally, and then sometime later struggled with shooting pains into my right calf. My chiropractor decided to do x-rays and searched my spine. What he found was a tiny fracture in my lower back that we traced back to a skiing accident when I was a teenager.

Without having that information, I was doing internet searches and fearing I had a blood clot, but since my chiropractor searched me and knew what was causing my turmoil, he was able to give me core-strengthening exercises to help. And it has helped immensely. I am stronger now and seldom have any symptoms.

> I HAVE TO STAY WILLING TO HAVE GOD SEARCH MY HEART FOR FRACTURES IN MY SOUL

In the same way, I have to stay willing to have God search my heart for fractures in my soul. And then to follow His guidance in knowing the truth and applying whatever He leads me to for healing, knowing that He is gentle and humble in heart.

Some ideas that can be healing for our soul that we can incorporate into our lives:

Music (listening/singing)
Bible reading
Memorize Scripture verses
Books
Audio teachings/programs
Solitude/silence (e.g., sitting quietly in nature)

Journaling

Turn off the tv

Feel ALL of your emotions

Prayer—just talking to God like a friend

    Vital prayer: "God, keep my heart soft and open to You/Your Truth."

Testimony of others (no comparing yourself!)

Walking/other physical exercise

Improved nutrition

Add supplements

Emotionally healthy relationships/support

    Vital reminder: People can never meet all your needs!

Self-care

Possibly seek medical treatment

Possibly seek counseling

THE ME THAT GOD INTENDED

Jesus said, "'I am the resurrection and the life.'" (John 11.25) He had to die before He could be that. I want to be resurrected from the rubble in my life. From the things that lack peace in my life. From the things that are disrupted. I want to really experience life as God intended. But just like with Jesus, something in me has to die. When Jesus died, it was all of our sins that He had taken upon Himself that were put to death on the cross. Whatever is not as it should be in me now also needs to be put to death before there can be resurrection to new life.

There is underlying anxiety in me. I want to get to the root of it. Where there is worry and anxiety, it is not of God. And whatever is not of God, I want that to be put to death so I can have life. Where there is fear, I want to allow God to put to death the cause of my fear so that I can be resurrected to new life.

Lord, whatever You want to use to bring death to anything that is not aligned with You, help me to be wise and humble in bringing these things to You and laying them at Your feet. Give me Your truth and a heart that is willing to hear anything You want to speak or do in order to align with You and live a life of freedom as You intended.

24

PLAN 'B'

"We can make our plans,
but the Lord determines our steps."
–Proverbs 16.9, NLT

y friend, Lillian, and I were planning to get away to my parents' river house for a couple days for some refreshment. We had been pouring ourselves out in ministry and needed time to rest, enjoy God and have some fun.

We got to the river house late in the evening on the first day and got settled. My plan was for us to drive my parents' fun little Geo convertible into town and spend a couple hours walking through Dow Gardens (110 acres of beautiful and uniquely landscaped gardens). It would be our only full day in town and the following day we would have to head back home.

I kept checking the weather forecast. It was calling for rain part of the day, but as I kept checking, the chance of rain kept increasing. I was stressing out since my plan was important to me, but even more importantly, I wanted to provide this refreshment for Lillian. I knew the plan would delight and refresh her.

I kept hoping and praying that my plan would work out and that even if it rained for a bit in the morning, it would clear up so we could leave around noon and be able to confidently drive the convertible into town in the sunshine and then have a lovely, sunny walk through the gardens. It was a good plan! I was hoping God would understand how good of a plan it was and make sure that we had a sunny afternoon. I planned on Him recognizing the good plan and bringing it about—after all, my motives were good in that I wanted this "gift" for my friend.

I woke up the next morning to heavy rain. I immediately grabbed my phone to check the hourly forecast: 70% - 100% chance of rain and thundershowers for the next 24 hours. I was immediately distraught. Why wouldn't God provide for such a good plan? I was so discouraged, and I told Lillian, as I was nearly in tears, about my disappointment and that I really wanted to give her the kind of refreshing day we had planned.

I noticed how peaceful she was. She said, "We'll just have to figure out Plan B and see what God has for us today." She let me know that just getting away, regardless of what we're doing, is refreshing for her. What really impacted me, though, was knowing how much she loved our plan, yet was so peaceful with seeing what Plan B would look like. I even saw a sense of excited anticipation about what God's Plan—our Plan B would end up being.

As it turned out, we had some amazing quiet time with God through the morning, and we were able to share with each other what God was teaching us, and it was beautiful. Then, despite the rain, we decided to drive (not the convertible though) into town. As we arrived in town, the weather actually cleared, and we decided to go walk through Dow Gardens. We were able to spend a delightful two hours there, and just as we were finishing up our time there, walking out of the rose garden, it started to lightly sprinkle. We had done all that we desired there and walked back to my car. As soon as we got to my car, the rain began to pour. And my heart was overwhelmed with God's grace.

What I learned that day was that I can make my plans, but God may have a Plan B. When He does, I can be assured that His plans are good:

"'For I know the plans I have for you,' declares the Lord, 'plans to prosper you and not to harm you, plans to give you hope and a future.'" (Jeremiah 29.11)

BE A DANIEL

Although times of fun and refreshment are necessary and good, sometimes the circumstances are a little more serious. I was drawn to read the book of Daniel. He was "a stranger in a strange land...during a time when the Jewish people seemed to have little hope." (From the

Intro in my Bible.) The people of Judah, as well as their king, were unfaithful to the Lord (1 Chronicles 9.1 and 2 Kings 24.19). The people gradually became desensitized to wrongdoing and no longer made faithfulness to God a priority. As a result, the Lord gave an ungodly king victory over Judah. This ungodly king did some good things, yet did not have God's favor, and without God's favor, a nation is left to its own devices and propels itself into corruption and destruction. Daniel, however, "made up his mind not to defile himself" with the king's agenda. At times he was respected, other times he was sentenced to death. At all times, though, God showed him favor and sustained and blessed his life, even in the midst of an unfavored nation.

I'm guessing that having favor with the king was probably Daniel's Plan A, but Daniel had convictions before God and stood by those convictions in his faithfulness to God. Things didn't go as he had hoped, yet God was with him through it all, giving him favor.

When we choose faithfulness to God above all else—above freedoms and privileges—despite difficulties and persecutions that may arise as a result, we can rest in God's favor and have a heart at peace. That is worth everything. Be a Daniel!

25

REFLECTIONS, DEPTHS & DIRT

"As water reflects the face,
so one's life reflects the heart."
–Proverbs 27.19

A SINGLE BANANA

*R*eflections. I want to be a reflection of Christ to the world around me. Yet I fall so far short.

I mentioned at the beginning of this book that I had been in Chicago taking a week to compile this book. I took the train there from Michigan and didn't have a car, so I just walked wherever I needed to go nearby.

One morning I was spending some time with God and reading a devotional from Kathy Troccoli. It inspired me to pray and ask God to make me a reflection of Him, and then I left the hotel to walk several blocks to a store.

Well, there were homeless people everywhere there. It was hard to walk down one city block and not see at least one or two. It grieved my heart.

There was a man begging for change as I walked into a store. I told him I would see what I have when I come out. While I was in the store, I got some bananas and I got one for him too, but when I came out, I was sad because he was gone. Instead there was a homeless woman sitting in his place. She looked up holding her change cup, and I asked her if she would like a banana. You'd think I had given her a $100 bill. She was so grateful—blessing me and my day! It gripped my heart.

Before I left my hotel room, I had prayed asking God to help me to be a reflection of Him. As it turned out, I gave a woman a single, 19 cent banana, and I was the one that was blessed.

Jesus said, "'The poor you will always have with you, but you will not always have me.'" (Matthew 26.11) He recognized the significance of time with Him. When I keep time with Him as my priority, I can then be infused with His love and His character to then go out into the world and reflect what He has infused in me—receiving His love and reflecting that love to others. When I live like I'm loved, I can then show others how much they're loved as well. And as a result, there will be less soul-poorness in our midst.

DEPTHS OF LOVE

God is able to take our little acts of obedience (regardless of how successful we view them) and do His great work. I had been talking to my then 15-year-old son about this, and he reminded me of David's obedience with hurling a stone at Goliath, and Joshua circling the wall and blowing a horn (and the great impact that God brought about as a result).

"But when anything that's shattered is laid before the Lord, just watch and see, it will not be unredeemed." -Selah (from the song "Unredeemed")

One line in the song, "Son of God" by Starfield, states, "You alone were broken on the altar of love." As I pondered that line and the pain I have felt at times in my (albeit imperfect) attempts to love others, I felt strength to continue on because I was struck by God's ability to relate perfectly to my pain. Choosing to love can be painful at times. When I choose to love, I choose to make myself vulnerable to accomplish whatever it is that God wants to accomplish in love. Love sees the value in the recipient of love and is willing to lay down its own will, desires, timeline, justice, perspective and standards so that the recipient can experience the depths of love. There is deep joy in being a part of that kind of scenario.

What do the depths of love look like? The depths of love look like...

- ✓ grace...to give beauty without reason.
- ✓ mercy...to give freedom where there is guilt, because "love covers a multitude of sins." (1 Peter 4.8b, NLT)
- ✓ patience...to compassionately wait while beauty takes form.
- ✓ kindness...to display honor because amazing intrinsic value is recognized.
- ✓ forgiveness...to not remember or bring forth former wrongs since God will crush them completely at the right time.
- ✓ believing the best (what's true, honorable and right)...to recognize that the big picture isn't always evident, and what "appears" to be, may be skewed.
- ✓ gentleness...to pursue understanding where wounds have been formed.
- ✓ joy...to reveal a conviction of a deeper hope.
- ✓ pursuit...to move toward and be convinced of the great and unique beauty and worth that has purpose to transform when fully realized.

- ✓ faithfulness...to never give up or lose hope because God is not finished and is still at work.
- ✓ peace...to be able to "be still" with the knowledge that neither of us is yet complete, but still wholly accepted and overcome by God's love.

HOW'S YOUR SOIL?

I'm thinking through the Parable of the Sower (a.k.a., the Story of the Farmer Scattering Seed). I'm thinking through it in detail. The seed is God's message. Did you notice in the parable that the soil is you and me—not our circumstances?

THE SOIL IS YOU AND ME — NOT OUR CIRCUMSTANCES

How the seed grows in us is determined by US.
Look at the characteristics of each type of soil.

GOOD SOIL = those who:
- are honest
- are good hearted
- hear God's message/Word
- accept God's message
- apply understanding of God's message/Word
- "cling" to it; patiently holding on

THORNY SOIL = those who:
- hear God's message
- accept God's message
- are distracted by cares of this life
- are distracted by making money/finances
- are distracted by pleasures

ROCKY SOIL = those who:
- hear God's message with joy
- they're excited, but the excitement hasn't penetrated their heart much beyond an emotional response. So when a difficult emotion takes over, they're gone

HARD PATH = those who:
- hear God's message
- don't understand/believe it because Satan has blinded them from seeing truth/deceived them into thinking that God is wrong

WHAT'S YOUR FOUNDATION?

Along the same lines, you've probably heard the parable about the man who built his house on the rock, a solid foundation, vs. the man who built his house on sand, and it collapsed. There is actually only ONE difference between the two men.

Jesus said that both men came to Him. Both men listened to Him. BOTH (probably sincerely) wanted to know what He had to say.

Maybe in our culture and society today, it might be like going to church every Sunday, having Quiet Times with God in order to read and hear His Word to really KNOW it.

The ONLY difference in them was that one obeyed and applied what he learned, and the other did not.

It's much like those who learn all about healthy eating and being physically fit. They understand all about it, and can probably even tell others all about how to be healthy, but their bodies collapse under the physical weight of pounds and disease, because they didn't apply what they learned.

Jesus said the only difference between a strong foundation with a house that stands strong, and a weak foundation with a house that "crumbles into a heap of ruins" is obedience.

What is the soil of your heart like? Build a strong foundation as you:

✓ apply understanding of God's message/Word
✓ "cling" to it; patiently holding on

26

LOOKING
(for the)
GOOD

"A joyful heart makes a cheerful face."
–Proverbs 15.13a, NASB

y husband and I wanted to take a break from a long, cold Michigan winter with a volatile spring that had a lot of cold and rainy days, and go someplace warm, solitary (for good God-time and writing time), peaceful and delightful, so we came down to a beach house in Florida that was given to us for a week. This impressive 3-story house is right on the Atlantic Ocean with a beautiful view all up and down the beach. This beach house is 5000 square feet with 7 bedrooms, 2 kitchens, 4 bathrooms, a sprawling second floor with a great room, fireplace, huge fully-furnished kitchen, two dining tables, a 30-foot wall of windows facing the ocean leading to the balcony overlooking a tremendous view of the ocean. And then the third floor has a 1000 square foot master suite that includes a king bed, fireplace, wet bar, dining nook, jacuzzi, recliners, large flat screen tv, two large walk-in closets, 50 feet of ocean-facing windows with a glass door wall leading to the balcony providing chairs to view spectacular sunrises.

Sounds amazing, doesn't it? And it is. As I write, I'm sitting in the dining nook in the master suite nearly surrounded by windows, and most of what I see is water and waves crashing in and rolling up on the sandy beach.

Now, tell me if the awe and wonder of your perception would be swayed if I filled in some more details, such as:

- The weather is cool, windy and wet.
- It has been overcast and raining since we arrived and is expected to continue raining (80 - 100% chance) constantly the entire week that we are here—no sun at all.
- All the blinds in the entire house have been taken down (and are lying on the floor in each room) and the morning light comes in at 6:30am, and the new blinds are not here yet.
- The air smells like fish.
- The first bed where I was sleeping caused my back to ache.
- The door wall in the master suite is leaking and allowing the rain to come in and soak the carpet in a 10x5 foot area.

- A contractor and his brother came this morning and will be here all day today (as well as four of the six days we will be here), and they will be painting, hammering, repairing the door wall in the master suite and doing work all through the house on every level.
- The normally-beautiful, sandy beach is currently mostly black and cluttered with ocean weeds and debris that has washed up on it.
- All the new windows still have ugly stickers on them.
- There are power lines cluttering my view.
- The wind is blowing the rain against windows and obstructing the view.
- And the nearest Starbucks is 20 minutes away!

Does it make you feel any different?

I know I will be deeply influenced by whatever I allow my mind to dwell on. If I choose to dwell on the several bullet points above, I will get discouraged and be grumpy and probably have a miserable time this week. However, if I choose to dwell on every one of the amazing gifts relating to this trip, my heart will overflow with blessing and awe and delight at how much I've been given. Look at all the amazing gifts I've been given in the first paragraph of this chapter! I am so very blessed! And as I sit here in this dining nook, I'm able to write comfortably, use Wi-fi, watch the ocean waves, watch the seagulls and an occasional heron flying nearby, and even occasionally open the door wall and listen to the waves. And I barely notice that the contractors are here.

I need to apply this to the rest of my life as well. As perfect as we think things have the potential of being, nothing in this world, of course, is perfect. We set ourselves up for failure when we expect a life without inconvenience, without pain, without wind and waves and clutter and obstructed views. I think we naturally gravitate toward and long for beauty—after all, we were created to live in a Garden. When I post pictures on Facebook of the majestic waves or the beauty of this beach house, it can be easy to be deceived and think everything is perfect. It can give way to discouragement, jealousy and frustration. When we allow the imperfections (or the things we want and don't have) to steal our joy, it depletes us of life.

But Jesus said, "'I came so they can have real and eternal life, more and better life than they ever dreamed of.'" (John 10.10b, MSG)

So how do we maintain joy and life, and even have "'better life than [we] ever dreamed of'"?

God's Word, of course, gives us guidance. In Philippians 4.8 and 12 (NLT), it says,

8 "...Fix your thoughts on what is true, and honorable, and right, and pure, and lovely, and admirable. Think about things that are excellent and worthy of praise."

12 "I know how to live on almost nothing or with everything. I have learned the secret of living in every situation, whether it is with a full stomach or empty, with plenty or little."

The chapter title is "LOOKING (for the) GOOD". When you are choosing to roll with the negative bullet points, and consciously "looking for the good" in all of your circumstances—fixing your thoughts on what is good and right, etc., the result will impact your countenance and your behavior—and it will keep you LOOKING GOOD.

A MODEL

Another thing that will help keep us looking good is when we remember Who it is that we can model our lives after. When things in my life aren't looking so good, I want to remember that my God…

- is a strong fortress
- is a strong deliverer
- is an ever-present help in trouble
- is my refuge and strength
- is my defender
- is my God of hope
- is my God who can scale a mountain
- is my redeemer
- is my provider
- goes before me
- makes the rough roads smooth

When I remember who HE is, I can pursue following in His footsteps in order to resemble my Father.

27

FINGERPRINTS

"'These stones are to be a memorial to
the people of Israel forever.'"
–Joshua 4.7b

o you know that God is cheering you on? He wants you to succeed in the beautiful plans He has for your life. He wants you to live victoriously.

Listen to this, written by a man who knew God well:

"You have made a wide path for my feet to keep them from slipping." (Psalm 18.36, NLT)

God doesn't want you to slip, so He widens your options to empower you and give you opportunity to accomplish what's right, to make good choices when you're tempted, to help someone else when you feel selfish, to have someone or something to grab onto when you're about to fall, to notice something to smile about when you want to harm someone else. If God wanted us to fail, He would have us walk a balance beam. In all honesty, sometimes it does feel that way; however, I also have to recognize that when I feel like I'm walking on a balance beam, it's often because I'm either setting rules for myself that God didn't OR I'm trying to walk the fine line between right and wrong rather than choosing to run on the right path. When I choose to look toward the right path, I begin to notice it widening.

FINGERPRINTS ON MY HEART

I must confess that I am often selfishly driven. I know much of my motivation in wanting to surrender to God is because I know that His plans are for good—and I want what's good for me. I want what brings me joy. I want what brings me peace. I believe God designed us to enjoy blessing as we surrender and serve and love, but I don't think He designed it for the blessing to be the motivation. I think He intended for His love to be the motivation regardless of blessings, gifts, prosperity, great health, no relational strain, the closest parking spot and an easy life.

I think of parents who work hard to provide for their family but may not have much, materially speaking, and their kids may have worn out clothes and the kids may even be ridiculed because of it, but those parents have an extravagant love for each other and for those kids— love that's not about "things", but it's about what really matters—what's lasting: character, doing what's best, and living out purpose and beautiful relationship. That's what I believe God's love for me is like, but He also throws in many blessings. He leaves His fingerprints all over my heart through His character expressed in many ways, including His blessings. Those parents also leave beautiful fingerprints on their children's hearts.

I want to leave those kinds of fingerprints—to love and serve because of how God has loved me—directly and through others. He loves me so much that He will sacrifice everything He has and pour Himself out completely for my benefit. His and others' fingerprints are always on my heart.

FINGERPRINTS ON THE HEARTS OF OTHERS

I like to visit cemeteries—especially old ones. I haven't always been like this, and I'm not really sure when it started.

But while I'm there, the world slows down. I don't feel pressure to "do". There's no performance needed. At a cemetery, I can just be. It's a peaceful place where I can relax and just be able to think for as long as I want. At a cemetery, the noise of the world becomes quieted and I can more easily connect with God. I need all of that.

But it's more than that. Human lives are buried there—people with stories and experience and wisdom. People who've touched the lives of others and left their fingerprints on the hearts and lives of many. Certainly, not all fingerprints have been good, but when the stories and experiences have been guided or redeemed by God, they become a testimony to God's faithfulness and beauty.

Unless those who have passed shared their stories in a way that would carry on through the years, most stories have been silenced. In the Old Testament, God had His people build "standing stones"—pillars—to mark a certain location as a reminder of a story that would be passed on for generations. He instructed them to keep sharing the stories—stories of His faithfulness to them so that future generations could be spiritually strengthened and know the love and faithfulness of God.

I wish we could know the stories behind each one of the stone markers in the cemetery. I wonder how many would be markers of God's faithfulness.

> WHAT FINGERPRINTS ARE WE LEAVING ON THE HEARTS OF OTHERS?

It causes me to stop and think... What markers are we leaving as testimonies to God's faithfulness for future generations? What fingerprints are we leaving on the hearts of others? What markers are we leaving as testimonies to the safety, security and freedom we've found in God?

GOD'S EXPRESSION

There was a poem I read once called:

"WITH THAT MOON LANGUAGE" by Hafez (14th century Persian poet)

Admit something:
Everyone you see, you say to them, "Love me."
Of course you do not do this out loud, otherwise someone would call the cops.
Still, though, think about this: this great pull in us to connect.
Why not become the one who lives with a moon in each eye, that is always saying,
with that sweet moon language,
what every other eye in this world is dying to hear?

I had been struggling with a desire to feel loved. God impressed on my heart that the only way others can love me well is by knowing very well His love for them (i.e., "We love because he first loved us." 1 John 4.19). People need our love. And His love is most often revealed to others through us.

As much as I want to be loved, the experience of love happens for us through those who experience love (i.e., God loving us through others, and God loving them through others—or some source of His choice). I am called to love, but beyond this, people most commonly love (and enjoy) those who love well. God is love, and we are drawn to manifestations of His love.

WE ARE DRAWN TO MANIFESTATIONS OF HIS LOVE

C.S. Lewis wrote this:

It is a serious thing to live in a society of possible gods and goddesses, to remember that the dullest and most uninteresting person you talk to may one day be a creature which, if you saw it now, you would be strongly tempted to worship, or else a horror and a corruption such as you now meet, if at all, only in a nightmare. All day long we are, in some degree, helping each other to one or the other of these destinations. It is in the light of these overwhelming possibilities, it is with the awe and the circumspection proper to them, that we should conduct all our dealings with one another, all friendships, all loves, all play, all politics. There are no ordinary people. You have never talked to a mere mortal. Nations, cultures, arts, civilizations – these are mortal, and their life is to ours as the life of a gnat. But it is immortals whom we joke with, work with, marry, snub and exploit – immortal horrors or everlasting splendors. This does not mean that we are to be perpetually solemn. We must play. But our merriment must be of that kind (and it is, in fact, the merriest kind) which exists between people who have, from the outset, taken each other seriously – no flippancy, no superiority, no presumption. And our charity must be a real and costly love, with deep feeling for the sins in spite of which we love the sinner – no mere tolerance or indulgence which parodies love as flippancy parodies merriment. (Lewis/The Weight of Glory)

When I allow God to love me perfectly how He chooses, I will be able to be a source of God's expression of love to a wounded, hurting world that many times hasn't experienced love. And God will fill me with His peace and love.

And when people feel loved, it brings out the best in them.

GOD'S VOICE RESOUNDING IN MY HEART

It was December several years ago, and I had been driving home one evening from celebrating a friend's birthday. It occurred to me that I had been feeling different for the past few days. I had gone through an entire year feeling heaviness and searching for relief.

As I thought about it, I recognized that my heart was lighter and had begun to soften as I had started reading Larry Crabb's book, 66 Love Letters, earlier in the week. And then even more as I anticipated an old friend coming to visit—that alone released something in my soul. I felt like I could just be me—in all my humanity and weakness and complete reality—KNOWING confidently that I would be unconditionally loved, embraced, touched, cherished, delighted in.

And I was. It reminded me (especially as she spoke of Song of Solomon) of how God sees me and feels about me—how He sees me in every aspect—in my completeness—and still greets me with, "Hi Beautiful!" It renewed and revived my heart for intimacy with Him... trust in Him... desperation for Him.

"You have the words of eternal life." (John 6.68b)

"You have made known to me the paths of life." (Acts 2.28a)

So as I was driving home after the birthday party, thinking about this, Chris Tomlin's song "Amazing Grace (My Chains are Gone)" came on the radio. I had never heard or experienced the words of that song as I did that night.

SOMETHING HAD BEEN HOLDING ME DOWN THAT WHOLE YEAR, AND I HAD A GROWING DESPERATION FOR RELIEF...

Something had been holding me down that whole year, and I had a growing desperation for relief from it through the whole year. I continued to spiral downward as I focused on finding relief. I finally recognized that I had spent much of the year desperate for relief—putting me in a bondage cycle.

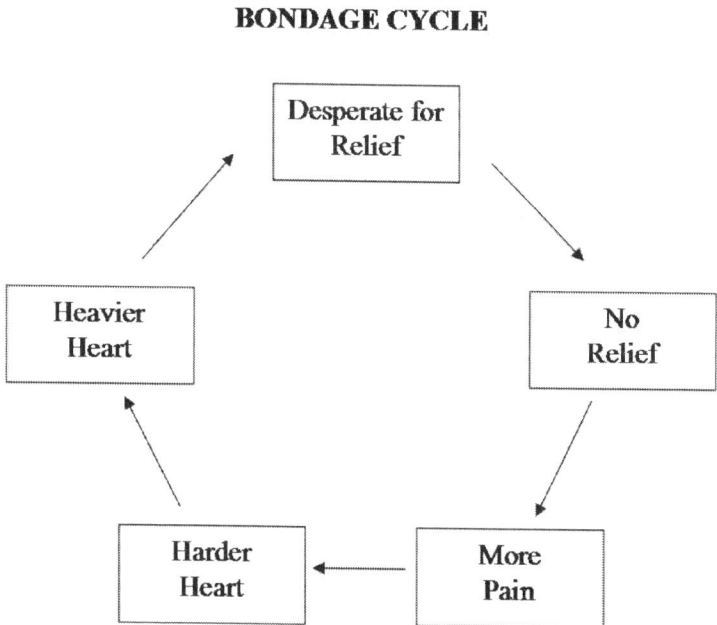

BONDAGE CYCLE

```
                    ┌──────────────┐
                    │ Desperate for│
                    │    Relief    │
                    └──────────────┘
        ↗                               ↘
┌──────────┐                      ┌──────────┐
│ Heavier  │                      │   No     │
│  Heart   │                      │ Relief   │
└──────────┘                      └──────────┘
     ↑                                 ↙
┌──────────┐      ┌──────────┐
│ Harder   │ ←─── │  More    │
│  Heart   │      │   Pain   │
└──────────┘      └──────────┘
```

What I really needed, though, was to be desperate for God, which would yield a freedom cycle.

FREEDOM CYCLE

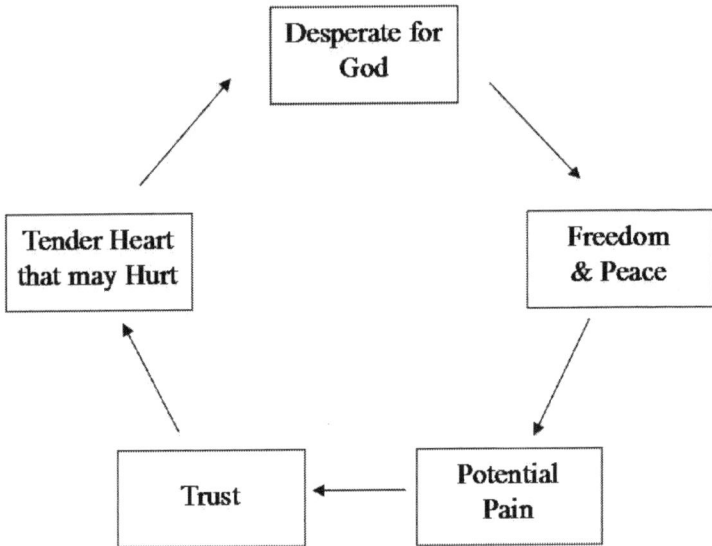

```
                    ┌──────────────┐
                    │ Desperate for│
                    │     God      │
                    └──────────────┘
        ↗                              ↘
┌──────────────┐                ┌──────────────┐
│ Tender Heart │                │   Freedom    │
│ that may Hurt│                │   & Peace    │
└──────────────┘                └──────────────┘
        ↑                              ↙
┌──────────────┐  ←──────  ┌──────────────┐
│              │           │  Potential   │
│    Trust     │           │    Pain      │
└──────────────┘           └──────────────┘
```

And as I drove home from the birthday party, I realized that my heart, having turned toward desperation for Him, trust in Him and intimacy with Him, was at peace. Bondage had been broken. My chains were gone, and I had been set free!

Just then I drove into the parking lot of a park near my house. My "Tree of Issues" was in front of me. This was the tree that God spoke to me about a few years earlier. I had been overwhelmed with all my issues, and God showed me that all those tiny branches representing all my issues were connected to bigger branches that are connected to bigger branches that are connected to bigger ones...and really there are just a few major issues—and when we deal with one major issue, hundreds of tiny issues disappear with it. A few days after the first time I saw the tree, I parked in a different place and saw the tree from a different angle. At the new angle, I could see that a huge section had been eliminated from the center of the tree.

MORE OF MY CHAINS WERE GONE, AND MORE OF ME HAD BEEN SET FREE!

That was three years earlier. On the night of the birthday party, as I parked in the first position, where the tree looked full of branches before, I now could see space in the middle—more branches were gone—more issues were resolved. More of my chains were gone, and more of me had been set free!

28

REDEMPTION SPECIALISTS

"They will rebuild the ancient ruins
and restore the places long devastated;
they will renew the ruined cities
that have been devastated for
generations."
–Isaiah 61.4

here was a knock on the door. It was 96° outside, and the maintenance man needed to switch out an air conditioning unit that wasn't cooling the room and bring me a new desk chair to replace the broken one.

This was only my second day in this hotel room and I had three more days here. I'm grateful for people who tend to maintenance issues, but it can be inconvenient. I'm here to write and be productive, but these issues are distracting. Last month, we were blessed with the beach house where we stayed in Florida for a week. It was wonderful although we did have to share it with the guys doing maintenance (painting, plumbing, replacing a door wall) during the day.

I think my tendency (and maybe yours too?) is to look at maintenance as an inconvenience. It takes extra time away from what I really want and need to be doing. On the other hand, God has already told us that we live in a fallen world—a world where things wear out and break down. So why am I so surprised and feel inconvenienced when maintenance needs to happen? Why am I slow to see it expectantly and so reluctant to see it as opportunity?

I changed my mindset this morning. I used the situation as an opportunity. Housekeeping came by and I chatted with Whitney—I don't know her official title, but I'm calling her a "Redemption Specialist"—she's the woman who made my room refreshing and inviting once again. It was refreshing and freeing to connect with the woman who could redeem my surroundings, and to have an opportunity to gaze through a window in her life to get to know her just a bit.

My life, too, needs maintenance. Something struck me this morning as I was reading in Acts 13. It says:

> Many Jews and godly converts to Judaism who worshiped at the synagogue followed Paul and Barnabas, and the two men urged them, "By God's grace, remain faithful."
>
> 45But when the Jewish leaders saw the crowds, they were jealous; so they slandered Paul and argued against whatever he said. Then Paul

and Barnabas spoke out boldly and declared, "It was necessary that this Good News from God be given first to you Jews. But since you have rejected it and judged yourselves unworthy of eternal life—well, we will offer it to Gentiles." (Acts 13.43, 45-46, NLT)

It seems to be that the Jewish leaders lacked maintenance. Soul and spirit maintenance keeps us tender-hearted, teachable, and evidencing the fruit of the spirit. I don't see this with the Jewish leaders. Those, however, who were pursuing soul and spirit maintenance were the ones who were following Paul and Barnabas and looking for life-transforming truth—not as a one-time clean-up, but as an ongoing practice.

> I NEED TO GET IN GOD'S WORD...SO THAT MY MIND WILL BE LIKE HIS

I know I need to get in God's Word and stay in it constantly so that my mind will be like His; otherwise, my mind becomes like my sinful nature and the nature of the world around me (because my ways are not God's ways—Isaiah 55.8b). That's the maintenance I need—and just like with Whitney this morning, that connection will be sweet and refreshing.

Maintenance isn't necessarily convenient, but it's critical. It's not natural, but it can be delightful and refreshing.

THE TOOL OF THE TASK

Speaking of inconvenience, I've hosted a garage sale fundraiser for the past ten years to help support LifeCare. From my limited perspective, I saw my purpose as collecting and pricing items, organizing a sale, selling items and raising money for the ministry. It took me a while before I recognized a broader purpose: allowing the sale to be a tool for impacting and caring for people—a tool that allowed me to be a "Redemption Specialist". God gave me the opportunity to host a practical event, but it was actually also a tool He would use to care for others. I noticed that at times, someone would come to my house to drop off sale items, and being focused, my tendency would be to quickly help them unload the items into my garage, give them a donations receipt and send them on their way. I've probably missed many opportunities through the years, until I began to recognize opportunities where I could be the hands and feet of Jesus for others. One friend came to drop off stuff, and as I noticed her lingering a bit, I invited her in and gave her a cold bottle of water to drink as she began sharing with me about her weariness in life. Hopefully, I was able to be a refreshment to her through that opportunity.

Another time, my friend, Renee, was talking about her job as a coach. She talked of how coaching may be her passion, but first, it's a tool for her to have a positive impact on kids and to share Jesus' love with them. That's her greater passion.

I know many of my friends have this perspective. Whether it's a job, a hobby, entertainment, ministry, a sporting event, a family gathering, shopping, relaxing or taking a class, don't be surprised by the "inconvenience" of a bigger purpose. God doesn't just focus on one task to check off the "To Do" list; He works "everything" together for good, as Romans 8.28 talks about, and will accomplish much (especially in caring for people) through the tool of the task as we allow Him to use us as "Redemption Specialists".

SCAPEGOAT

Did you know that a scapegoat was, biblically, in the Old Testament, an actual goat that bore people's sins and then was removed to the wilderness so as to remove people's sins from them? (Leviticus 16.10, "But the goat chosen by lot as the scapegoat shall be presented alive before the LORD to be used for making atonement by sending it into the wilderness as a scapegoat.") Today, we refer to people who are unfairly blamed for things as scapegoats. Do you ever feel like a scapegoat—blamed for things that really aren't even about you?

Sometimes I feel that way. I just came across something I had written in my journal a while back after reading about how Jesus was blamed: Martha blamed Jesus for Lazarus' death. Mary blamed Jesus for Lazarus' death—but Mary cried, and it moved Jesus' spirit and He was troubled. Even some of the Jews with them blamed Him. Then Jesus resurrected Lazarus.

So often I want to justify myself, clear my name and prove my innocence—and have nothing to do with being nice to my accusers. But the amazing thing about God's grace is that I don't see Him doing that. Instead, I see Him moving forward in love and grace that covers sin, even when it means entrusting His reputation and unjust accusations to His Father, understanding that "love covers over a multitude of sins." (1 Peter 4.8b) And it's in love that there is hope for redemption.

TREE OF HOPE

Many years ago, I first saw a particular tree at a park that I visit often near my house. (I wrote about it in the previous chapter regarding a time many years after my first visit.) I remember the first time I had parked right in front of that huge tree and how it looked full and beautiful.

I had been overwhelmed with all of my issues in my life, but God was teaching me that my issues are much like the branches of the tree. When we are able to get to some root issues (i.e., large branches), then a lot of the smaller issues naturally fall away.

Then he drew my attention to another side of the tree where it appeared that lightning may have struck it, and a huge branch was severed and gone. He was showing me that's what he's doing in my life, even though from where I was parked, you couldn't tell that any branches were missing.

A year or so later, I noticed that another large branch was gone, and you could kind of notice it a little bit from the parking lot. It was very encouraging to me and symbolized what God was continuing to do in my life.

Since then, the township has completely redesigned the park and the parking lot is no longer where it used to be. Over the last few years I hadn't even really paid attention to the tree, until this week. I've been coming here a lot the past month, but I feel like this week God has really drawn the tree to my attention. This time of the year, there are no leaves so the branches that are there are more noticeable. I sensed God was speaking to me about how He's continuing to work in me and bring redemption to my life as the lack of branches on my tree is so noticeable now. So I took a picture (from the same spot where the parking lot used to be).

GOD CONTINUES TO
BEAUTIFY MY LIFE
AND...WILL CONTINUE
TO DO SO UNTIL I AM
PERFECTED IN HIS
PRESENCE

I guess what encourages me is that on this side of Heaven, even though I will be incomplete—a work in progress, in His work, God continues to beautify my life and make me more like Him. He will continue to do so until I am perfected in His presence.

But our citizenship is in heaven. And we eagerly await a Savior from there, the Lord Jesus Christ, who, by the power that enables him to bring everything under his control, will transform our lowly bodies so that they will be like his glorious body. (Philippians 3:20-21)

29

PEOPLE WHO BITE

"A person's wisdom yields patience; it is
to one's glory to overlook an offense."
–Proverbs 19.11

everal years ago, we decided to adopt a sweet,
gentle, senior German Shepherd. Initially we
thought she was about eight years old, but the
vet determined her age to be closer to twelve, which is
about the average lifespan of a German Shepherd. The
"adoption agency" had named her Gwyn, and we
decided to keep the name. As we brought Gwyn into our
family, she had to learn all about us just as we had to
learn all about her.

We learned that she was very quiet, gentle, tender,
obedient, careful with her actions and followed me
everywhere, but one of the first main learning
experiences for me was understanding her abilities (and
disabilities). One of the first days I let her out into our
fenced in backyard, I opened the back door and I gently

guided her out onto the deck and down the three steps onto the grass. I then let her off the leash so she could roam and explore the backyard freely.

She did her business and then inquisitively and slowly explored the yard. I came back in the house for a bit, but I checked on her randomly. After a while, I checked on her and she was standing where the deck met the house, with a lilac bush on the other side of her, about ten feet from the steps. Not knowing her abilities, I called to her to jump up (about 18" or so) onto the deck to come in. She put her front paws up on the deck and was unsuccessfully trying to push herself up. Seeing her dilemma, I went out to lift her bottom up to give her a gentle push to help her make it up on the deck. As I did, she squealed and threw her head around as if she was about to bite me—the source of the pain she was feeling. I hadn't realized the extent of her arthritis in her hips, and when I touched her in a way that triggered pain, she lashed out, even though that wasn't her typical disposition.

People are that way too. They may lash out and try to bite us in various ways when we think we're just trying to be helpful. I think our typical response to people like that is to react similarly to the way they're mistreating us. But what if we recognized that the more they lash out, the more their pain is revealed? How would it impact our love, our compassion, our heart toward them?

With Gwyn, I knew her disposition was to be tender toward me and others, and when I realized her pain, my heart had compassion for her and looked for ways to help her feel safe, secure and free to live out her days that focused on her strengths and understood and helped accommodate for her weaknesses. When I recognized that she had physical limitations that prevented her from jumping up onto the deck, I led her back to the steps and empowered her to climb the steps back onto the deck—accomplishing the same goal, but with her abilities in mind.

When we seek to understand others' pain and weaknesses with compassion, we can provide a safe and secure environment and actually find ways to empower them to live with strength and freedom to accomplish all that God is calling them to.

EMPOWERING THE WEAK

There is a scene in the movie, *Mona Lisa Smile*, where Giselle walks into the room where two of her roommates are. Giselle begins to share with them how she spent the previous evening (in admittedly unwholesome ways). Betty, a former roommate, walks in and begins to condemn Giselle with accelerating contempt. Soon Giselle begins to walk out of the room as Betty's harsh berating gets more and more ugly. But Giselle stops, even in the midst of the escalating condemnation, turns back, walks right up to Betty and hugs her tightly. Betty begins to soften and then sobs painfully. Giselle and

Betty both understood the pain in Betty's heart from the betrayal she was experiencing in her marriage.

The more Betty lashed out, the more Giselle could see her pain, and the more she could respond wisely with love and compassion. Ultimately, Giselle's love provided a safe and secure place that empowered Betty to begin living with strength and freedom.

When we respond this way—embracing our own secure place in the arms of Jesus, we can then reflect God's character: "He gives strength to the weary and increases the power of the weak." (Isaiah 40.29)

30

BEAUTIFUL INCONVENIENCE

"'You are the God who sees me'"
–Genesis 16.13

The white piece of paper tucked into my driver's side window drew my attention. My first thought was that I got a parking ticket, even though I've parked in this open, public parking lot at a park at various times throughout the past 30 years without incident. My second thought was, *Why would a parking ticket be tucked in the side window rather than on the windshield?*

As I walked up to my driver's door, I was focused on the paper and business card of a police officer. Confused, I was trying to wrap my mind around and understand the paper I was looking at when I heard, "Excuse me." It was a woman's voice, but I was sure it wasn't for me. Then once again, "Excuse me." I turned around, still holding the white paper and trying to understand what I was reading and what it had to do with where I was parked.

A woman in her early thirties was approaching me. "I am so sorry I hit your car. I've been waiting for you to come back."

I was still struggling to make sense of what I thought was a parking issue, but I was starting to realize something different.

She looked distraught. I'm sure I looked confused. She motioned toward the large dent in my driver's door. I must have missed it before because I was so focused on the white paper on the window. I looked down at the paper I was holding and then back at her and asked if she had called the police.

She said, "Yes. There was actually another car that did the same thing that I did and backed into another car, but they drove away. So I went after them and called the police. They came and dealt with the hit-and-run issue, and then I told them about me hitting your car. After they left, I just waited here for you."

I could hardly believe she waited! I said, "Wow. That shows me you have a lot of integrity."

She again apologized profusely. I told her, "It's okay; accidents happen. We should probably exchange information."

I walked to my car door and realized I could only open it a couple inches because of the damage. When she realized this, she felt even worse. So I went around to the passenger's side and sat down. I asked her to come over to that side, and we exchanged all of our information. Again, she said, "I'm so sorry."

I said, "It's okay. We'll take care of it. Is your car okay?"

She pointed to the bumper and told me it's a leased vehicle but there was only a small amount of damage on the bumper.

She still seemed distraught, but we finally went our separate ways.

The next morning was Monday and I sent pictures and information to our insurance guy, but before I got a response, her insurance company called me. They said they would be covering the repairs for my car and would get me a rental vehicle in the meantime.

I realized I was a "victim" in this, and I was inconvenienced in it, and yet I watched God wrap His arms around me and love me in beautiful ways through each step in the situation. It kind of sounds silly, but I felt loved and cared for by every person involved in this! I have never ever had an experience like this or heard of anyone with an experience like this.

I only had to make one phone call regarding the whole situation, and that was to set up a time with the collision shop, and that appointment was only three hours from when I called them. When I got to the collision shop they told me realistically it would be Friday before they could get the quotes for the insurance company that they needed and then they would probably not even start on it till Monday, so I could still drive my car until then. When I told her that I couldn't open my driver's door and I had to climb over the passenger's seat to get in and out, she immediately said that it wasn't safe for me to drive, and I could leave the car with them and they would call the rental car place for me and have them come pick me up to go get my rental car immediately. (Because of how the insurance works, I couldn't get the rental until I left my car at the collision shop.) So when I got the rental car, I asked them how long I could keep it, and the guy said that the collision shop will be communicating with the insurance company and I would have the rental until my car is done—however long that takes, at which point I would drop off the rental and they would take me to my car.

On Wednesday, two days later, the collision shop called me and said that they already had the new door for my car and it was already being painted, and that there was a possibility I may have it back by Friday! She said she just wanted to keep me in the loop. I was shocked. They weren't even expecting to start on it till the following week!

Then on Thursday, she called me again to give me another update saying that it's very likely that it will be ready Friday afternoon.

There are times when we just need to experience God's love for us. Sometimes it happens in the most unexpected ways—an inconvenience, an accident, a detour. It sounds strange, but it felt like the girl who hit my car was an angel. And God was just beautifully loving and caring for me through all those people—and in an odd way, making me feel safe, secure and free.

31

THE OUTCOME

"And let us run with perseverance the
race marked out for us, fixing our eyes on
Jesus, the pioneer and perfecter of faith."
–Hebrews 12.1b-2a

As I've written this book, I've asked God several
questions:

- Do You keep people safe?
- Is it Your plan for people to have security—
  even in You?
- And do You want us to live in freedom?

Show me in Your Word how this is true if it is.

Something that has stood out to me is that this world
is not our home, and in this world, we are incomplete.
This body is not our safety and security. This body isn't
even life in its truest sense—it doesn't contain true life

nor does the world surrounding me. True life is what I will experience when I'm standing face-to-face with Jesus in the environment where He resides—not inhibited by the fallen world. Remember the Carnival I talked about in Chapter 2? There is so much more to our existence than these few years we have in this body.

THERE IS SO MUCH MORE

As we walk through this life, it is filled with uncertainty, at least for us. We walk into every situation not knowing the outcome. When God leads us to walk by faith, He's longing to guide us through this life because He sees the big picture. He's not bound by time, so He's already been to the future to know how to work it out. By faith we believe that we will remain in God's sovereignty regardless of what we see and regardless of the outcome in this part of our existence.

Joseph was sold into slavery. (Genesis 37) He didn't know what the outcome would be.

Esther went to the king in a forbidden way, risking her life for her people. (Esther 4-5) She didn't know what the outcome would be.

Shadrach, Meshach and Abednego refused to bow to worship a golden idol, so they were tied up and thrown into a scorching furnace that had been heated to seven times hotter than normal—so hot that it killed the soldiers that threw them in. (Daniel 3) They didn't know what the outcome would be.

David's life was in jeopardy because King Saul was jealous and wanted to kill him. (1 Samuel 19) He didn't know what the outcome would be.

Daniel walked by faith when he prayed to God when it was not allowed because the king's officials had conspired against him. (Daniel 6) He didn't know what the outcome would be.

Daniel was thrown into a lion's den because he was faithful to God and wouldn't worship the king. (Daniel 6) He didn't know what the outcome would be.

Jonah was thrown into the raging Mediterranean Sea. (Jonah 1) He didn't know what the outcome would be.

Stephen was faithful to God while some of the Jewish leaders conspired against him to kill him. (Acts 7) He didn't know what the outcome would be.

Paul was imprisoned many times. He didn't know what the outcome would be.

The martyrs didn't know what the outcome would be.

Lazarus was sick and died. (John 11) Neither he, nor his sisters, knew what the outcome would be.

We know who can stand in a lion's den with us and hold a lion's mouth closed. We know who can stand in a fiery furnace with us and surround us with a protective shield. We know who can unlock prison doors, calm seas and protect a man inside a great fish. We know who can give us favor, comfort and direction. We know who can give us peace in trials; and we know who can revive us. We know who can walk us into eternity when our time here is complete.

The experience of true life begins to happen when I can let go of fearfully protecting myself—when I can let go of fearfully keeping myself safe and secure. [A word of caution here, though. If you are in an unsafe situation or you sense that you are being treated in a way that you shouldn't be, please get wise counsel about your specific situation.]

That said, we must discern God's leading. There are times when danger will surround us. In this life we have limitations. But we were not created for this world. When we trust in Jesus, He will one day bring us to that world that we were created for. But here, with limitations to freedom and

HE DOES INCREDIBLY AMAZING WORK USING THINGS THAT ARE CORRUPT AND AWFUL

safety and security, we still have great purpose, and we are promised His companionship as we walk through trials. We are promised His wisdom as we navigate through those trials. We are promised His sovereignty that He will bring about good despite the trials, and even use the trials to make them align with His purpose and good plan. He does incredibly amazing work using things that are corrupt and awful. Even when Jesus was nailed to a cross, "God used the problem of people's sin to solve the problem of people's sin. He used the problem to solve the problem." (Shirock)

If He can do that, that's the side that I want to be on. It may not be pain-free, but it is filled with freedom, and when we finish our race here on earth, we will have perfect safety, security and freedom. But we must run this race with endurance.

"And let us run with perseverance the race marked out for us, fixing our eyes on Jesus, the pioneer and perfecter of faith." (Hebrews 12.1b-2a)

One final word: you need to know that this world will beat you up, BUT God created you to impact this world in a unique way. He's given you gifts, talents, certain traits, circumstances, preferences, etc., and guarded those in your life, so that they equip you perfectly to make a difference...for such a time as this. That makes you exceptional! And understanding the truth of who you are, and Whose you are, can make you safe and secure beyond human understanding, and it can set you free.

AFTERWORD

KELLY HAS ONCE AGAIN PROVIDED a way for others to experience her inner life, devotion to God and her intimate times with Him. I trust that you have not only enjoyed this book but savored her words as you were drawn into your own personal, deeper pursuit of God. He is our safe place. He is our security. He is our freedom.

If this book has left you longing for more, it has accomplished what I believe Kelly and those of us at LifeCare desire for you. Life is a journey, and we are thankful to have been part of so many people's healing process and growth over the years.

Kelly beautifully expresses all she has learned, and continues to give to others. We invite you to continue the journey whether it be through the pathways we provide at LifeCare or other pathways. Don't stop now— keep healing, growing and pursuing THE ONE who provides the only safety, security and freedom that LASTS!

–Lillian Easterly-Smith
Founder & Director, LifeCare Christian Center

WHAT IS LIFECARE?

LIFECARE CHRISTIAN CENTER is a nonprofit, inter-denominational organization in the service of providing individuals and families in the community with physical, spiritual, emotional and relational support while walking through life's challenges. We all have gone through life crises or at least know someone who has. LifeCare is for those who have a desire to overcome issues of the heart, learn life skills, and have a longing to change. At LifeCare, they find restoration, peace and purpose.

Founded by Lillian Easterly-Smith, LifeCare Christian Center provides a fresh and innovative approach to personal growth and healing by giving care and support to individuals and families within the community. LifeCare's mission is to offer opportunities for life transformation, and we strive to achieve this objective by providing a safe place of ongoing care and support for people of all ages from trained individuals who have been through similar life circumstances.

Lillian, herself, is an accomplished teacher, speaker and leader in the fields of Christian care, recovery and support group ministry with nearly three decades of experience.

LifeCare offers various opportunities for growth and healing. The following is a list of many of those opportunities:

- **Group Care** (care, support, recovery) A detailed list can be found on our web site.

- **Life Enrichment Opportunities** (workshops, seminars, classes, retreats)
  Anger, Stress, Abuse, Health & Wellness, Marriage Skills, Finances, Substance Abuse, Spiritual Growth

- **"The Great Exchange" –**
  Experiential Weekends for Women
  These weekends help women recognize who they are in Christ and experience healing, growth and truth that is life transforming. It's a safe place to be real and experience God.

- **"The Great Exchange" for Couples –**
  Living & Loving in a Whole-Hearted Marriage
  Whether you want to enrich & strengthen, or find hope for a troubled relationship, you will benefit from this weekend on your journey toward intimacy and oneness (body, soul & spirit). This experiential weekend is like no other marriage retreat you have ever attended.

- **Pastoral / Chaplaincy Care**

- **Funerals, Weddings, Crisis Care, etc.**

- **Life Coaching**
  Setting goals, planning & accountability accomplish results. Areas of focus are: career,

education, relational, spiritual growth and many other life issues. See possibilities! Set Priorities! Find the confidence to fulfill God's purpose for life!

- **Inner Healing Prayer Ministry**
  Opportunities for focused prayer to expose lies that cause painful emotions, allowing those lies to be replaced with truth.

- **Leadership Training & Development of Care & Support Ministries for Churches and Para-Church Organizations**

- **Professional Counseling**
  Searching for a competent, professional counselor with the same values as you? Our contracted professionals as well as those on our referral list have been screened and interviewed to be sure you will be receiving care and competent counseling from someone you can trust.

- **Professional Interventions** (addictions & compulsive behaviors) Based on the "Love First" approach.

- **Living Well**
  Classes and seminars for nutrition, exercise, and how to develop a healthy lifestyle.

Groups and life enrichment opportunities are offered periodically during the year. A full listing is available at www.lifecarechristiancenter.org.

LifeCare is a non-profit 501(c)3 organization and solely operates from charitable donations that are tax deductible.

REFERENCES

Abarim. http://www.abarim-
        publications.com/Dictionary/ay/ay-ts-
        b.html#.W_93ovZFzIU.

Boyle, Gregory. *Tattoos on the Heart*. New York: Free Press,
        2011.

Come Alive (Dry Bones). Lauren Daigle (written by Lauren
        Daigle and Michael Farren). UMG (on behalf of
        Centricity Music); Capitol CMG Publishing, Warner
        Chappell, CMRRA, AdRev Publishing, and 8 Music
        Rights Societies. 2014.

Crabb, Larry. *Inside Out*. Colorado Springs, CO: NavPress, 1988.

Forever Reign. Hillsong (on behalf of Hillsong Music and
        Resources LLC); ARESA, SOLAR Music Rights
        Management, ASCAP, Sony ATV Publishing, Adorando
        Publishing, CMRRA, Capitol CMG Publishing, UMPI,
        Essential Music Publishing, UMPG Publishing, and 21
        Music Rights Societies. 2012.

Free. https://www.merriam-webster.com/dictionary/free.

Hafiz. "With That Moon Language."
        https://www.servicespace.org/blog/view.php?id=12703.

Here As In Heaven. Elevation Worship (written by Chris
        Brown, Mack Brock, Matthew Ntlele, Steven Furtick,
        Wade Joye). 2016.

I Worship You, Almighty God. Don Moen (written by Sondra
        Corbett). Integrity, Hosanna! Music: 1992.

Lewis, C.S. *The Lion, the Witch and the Wardrobe*. New York:
        HarperCollins; Reprint edition, 2008.

Lewis, C.S. *The Weight of Glory*.
https://www.goodreads.com/quotes/282593-it-is-a-serious-thing-to-live-in-a-society.

Moore, Beth. "Freedom".
https://www.youtube.com/watch?v=KiC-kWF_WSY.

NACR. National Association for Christian Recovery daily devotional. Dale Ryan is an Associate Professor of Recovery Ministry at Fuller Theological Seminary. Juanita Ryan is a therapist in private practice. March 14, 2017.

O Come To The Altar. Elevation Worship. 2016.

Resurrecting. Elevation Worship (written by Chris Brown, Mack Brock, Matthew Ntlele, Steven Furtick, Wade Joye). 2017.

Safe. https://en.oxforddictionaries.com/definition/safe.

Safe. https://www.merriam-webster.com/dictionary/safe.

Secure. https://en.oxforddictionaries.com/definition/secure.

Shirock, Bob. Oak Pointe Church. December 2, 2018.

Studylight.
https://www.studylight.org/lexicons/hebrew/8312.html.

There Is A Cloud. Elevation Worship. Provident Label Group: 2017.

Troccoli, Kathy. *Live Like You Mean It*. Colorado Springs, CO: WaterBrook Press, 2006.

27670630R00143

Made in the USA
Lexington, KY
06 January 2019